Complications in Orthopaedics
Open Fractures

Edited by
L. Scott Levin, M
Paul B. Magnusson Pro.......... .. ..
    Joint Surgery
Chair, Department of Orthopaedic Surgery
University of Pennsylvania Health System
Philadelphia, Pennsylvania

Series Editor
Peter C. Amadio, MD
Mayo Clinic
Rochester, Minnesota

Published by the
American Academy of Orthopaedic Surgeons
6300 North River Road
Rosemont, IL 60018

AMERICAN ACADEMY OF ORTHOPAEDIC SURGEONS

American Academy of Orthopaedic Surgeons
6300 North River Road
Rosemont, IL 60018
1-800-626-6726

First Edition
Copyright © 2010 by the
American Academy of Orthopaedic Surgeons

ISBN   978-0-89203-639-4

Contributors

George Cierny III, MD
Senior Partner
REOrthopaedics, Inc.
San Diego, California

Janet D. Conway, MD
Director, Bone and Joint Infection
Rubin Institute for Advanced Orthopedics
Sinai Hospital of Baltimore
Baltimore, Maryland

Edward J. Harvey, MD, MSc
Chief of Trauma
Department of Orthopaedic Surgery
McGill University
Montreal, Canada

Marie-Noëlle Hébert-Blouin, MD
Fellow of Peripheral Nerve Surgery
Department of Neurologic Surgery
Mayo Clinic
Rochester, Minnesota

John E. Herzenberg, MD, FRCSC
*Director, International Center for Limb
    Lengthening*
Rubin Institute for Advanced Orthopedics
Sinai Hospital of Baltimore
Baltimore, Maryland

Marco Innocenti, MD
Director, Microsurgery Unit
Department of Orthopaedics
Careggi Hospital
Florence, Italy

Chih-Hung Lin, MD
Associate Professor and Chairman, Trauma
Department of Plastic and Reconstructive
    Surgery
Chang Gung Memorial Hospital
Taoyuan County, Taiwan

Salih Marangoz, MD
Attending Orthopaedic Surgeon
Department of Orthopaedic Surgery
Hacettepe University
Ankara, Turkey

Andrew N. Pollak, MD
Associate Director of Trauma
R. Adams Cowley Shock Trauma Center
Associate Professor and Head
Division of Orthopaedic Traumatology
University of Maryland School of Medicine
Baltimore, Maryland

Milan K. Sen, MD, FRCSC
Chief, Orthopaedic Trauma Service
Assistant Professor
Department of Orthopaedic Surgery
The University of Texas
    Health Science Center at Houston
Houston, Texas

Robert J. Spinner, MD
Professor
Department of Neurologic Surgery
Department of Orthopedic Surgery
Mayo Clinic
Rochester, Minnesota

Contents

Preface

Over the last half century, advances in fracture fixation and soft-tissue reconstruction have transformed the potential for limb salvage following severe extremity trauma. In addition, the evolution of orthopaedic trauma as a separate discipline within orthopaedics as well as landmark studies funded by the National Institutes of Health, such as the Lower Extremity Assessment Project (LEAP), have redefined the evaluation, treatment, and analysis of open fractures. New understandings about acquired infections and methicillin-resistant *Staphylococcus aureus*, innovations that have emerged during U.S. military engagements in Iraq and Afghanistan, and new technology such as the vacuum-assisted closure of wounds and dermal substitutes all have influenced greatly the treatment of open fractures. The application of technologic advances in bone and soft-tissue management also has optimized open fracture care, reducing the number of complications of open fractures.

Despite these advances, complications of open fractures still do occur. Some are preventable, and some will occur despite the best treatment. The surgeon who does not see complications is not operating and certainly is not taking difficult cases. This monograph discusses the prevention and management of the complications of open fractures from several vantage points, presented by the most respected clinicians in the field. Common decision-making errors in limb salvage are discussed by Dr. Andrew Pollak, who has gained inestimable experience at the R. Adams Cowley Shock Trauma Center at the University of Maryland School of Medicine and in treating the extremity war injuries seen in wounded warriors returning from active duty. The most daunting extremity injury considered for salvage is the so-called III C injury, the extremity with vascular injury. Dr. Chi-Hung Lin, a well-respected extremity traumatologist who is Chairman of Trauma at Chang Gung Memorial Hospital in Taoyuan, Taiwan, offers strategies to salvage seemingly unsalvageable extremities using the principles of damage-control resuscitation.

Dr. Edward Harvey, who is trained as a hand and microvascular surgeon and as an orthopaedic truamatologist and who has a unique perspective on the management of soft-tissue loss after trauma, discusses free-tissue transfers, negative pressure wound therapy, and dermal substitutes. Dr. Marco Innocenti, one of the world's leading experts on epiphyseal and vascularized bone transfer, provides algorithms for the management of bone loss. Infection is one of the most vexing problems in open fracture treatment. Dr. George Cierny presents his classification and treatment algorithm, which is one of the principal advances in the management of infection following open fractures. Dr. John Herzenberg's experience in limb lengthening and nonunions using the Ilizarov technique spans more than 25 years. He describes how the proper treatment of malunions and nonunions in the lower extremity can facilitate care and preserve limbs. Chronic pain following an open fracture—based on neuroma or chronic regional pain syndrome—often has been the cause of late amputations. This topic has been a career interest of Dr. Robert Spinner, who trained not only in orthopaedic surgery, but also in neurosurgery, and offers his expertise on the treatment of pain following open fractures. Through the discussion of cases provided by these leaders in the field of open fractures, this concise volume provides expert guidance on both the prevention and treatment of the complications of open fractures.

I would like to extend my appreciation to this distinguished international team of authors, who graciously committed their time and expertise to the publication of this monograph. I also would like to thank the staff of the Publications Department of the American Academy of Orthopaedic Surgeons, whose efforts made this publication a reality.

L. Scott Levin, MD, FACS
Editor

Chapter 1

Management of Bone Loss

L. Scott Levin, MD, FACS
Marco Innocenti, MD

CASE 1: OPEN FRACTURE OF THE HUMERUS

History

A 39-year-old woman presented with a 2-year history of recalcitrant nonunion following a Gustilo grade II open fracture of the left humerus. Primary treatment consisted of surgical débridement of the wound, reduction of the diaphyseal fracture, and bone fixation using external fixation. Six months later, upon evidence of a nonunion, the patient underwent a second operation, in which a cancellous bone graft was performed and a compression plate was used for fixation. One year after plating, a failure of the implant occurred, after minimal torque (**Figure 1**, *A*).

Current Problem

The patient presented with an angular deformity of the arm and severe functional impairment. The fracture was displaced and unstable, and the plate was tenting the skin. Furthermore, a palsy of the radial nerve, resulting from compression by the plate, was present. Radiographs showed a large area of osteoporotic and poorly vascularized bone with migration of the metal implant.

Case Management and Outcome

A lateral approach was chosen to expose the left humerus. The radial nerve was severely compressed by the plate, and a neurolysis was necessary to free the nerve from reactive fibrous tissue. After removal of the hardware, the quality of the bone was checked and serial resections of the proximal and distal stumps were performed until well-vascularized bone was reached, resulting in a 10-cm gap (**Figure 1**, *B*). A contralateral fibula graft was harvested and used to fill the defect. The bone fixation was accomplished with a low-contact plate (LCP) using unicortical screws in the fibular portion. Microvascular anastomoses were performed end to end to the deep brachial artery and the cephalic vein.

Neither of the following authors nor any immediate family members has received anything of value from or owns stock in a commercial company or institution related directly or indirectly to the subject of this article: Dr. Levin and Dr. Innocenti.

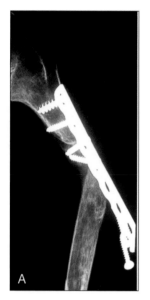  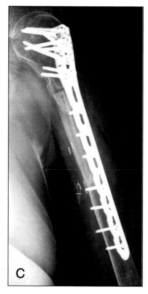 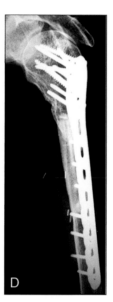

Figure 1 Recalcitrant nonunion following a Gustilo grade II open fracture of the left humerus in a 39-year-old woman. **A,** AP radiograph demonstrates the persistent nonunion and inadequate bone fixation that led to failure of the implant 1 year after surgery. **B,** Photograph taken after débridement of the fibrous tissue and nonvascularized bone demonstrates the final gap, which was 10 cm long (dotted arrow). A vascularized fibula graft was used to reconstruct the bone defect and was stabilized by an LCP. AP radiographs demonstrate the distal fusion (**C**) that occurred at 4 months and the fusion at the proximal junction (**D**) that was observed at 8 months after surgery.

Conventional reconstructive options include shortening of the humerus and replating, bone transportation techniques, and intercalary allografting. None of these procedures would have been able to manage the 10-cm defect created by the resection of the long segment of avascular bone.

After 4 months, the radial nerve had recovered almost completely and the distal osteotomy had healed (**Figure 1, C**). After 4 additional months, radiographs demonstrated bone fusion at the proximal junction (**Figure 1, D**).

CASE 2: OPEN FRACTURE OF THE RADIUS (LARGE GAP)
History

A 30-year-old man sustained a grade II open fracture of the left radius during a motor vehicle accident. The wound was débrided, and the fracture was reduced and fixed by a metal plate on the day of the accident.

After 1 year, no bone healing was observed, and the implant subsequently failed (**Figure 2, A**). The patient underwent a second surgery, during which a longer, more elastic plate was implanted and a cancellous bone graft was performed. This operation also resulted in failure. An atrophic pseudarthrosis developed, complicated by implant failure and bending of the plate (**Figure 2, B**).

Current Problem

This young, active patient reported pain, deformity, and severe limitation of pronation and supination of the hand. The failure of previous treatment resulted in shortening of the radius and angular deviation of the distal segment with subsequent loss of distal radioulnar joint (DRUJ) alignment.

Because of bone resorption, the actual shortening was even more extensive after the resection of the poorly vascularized diaphyseal segment. The only alternative to a one-bone forearm was a vascularized fibula graft.

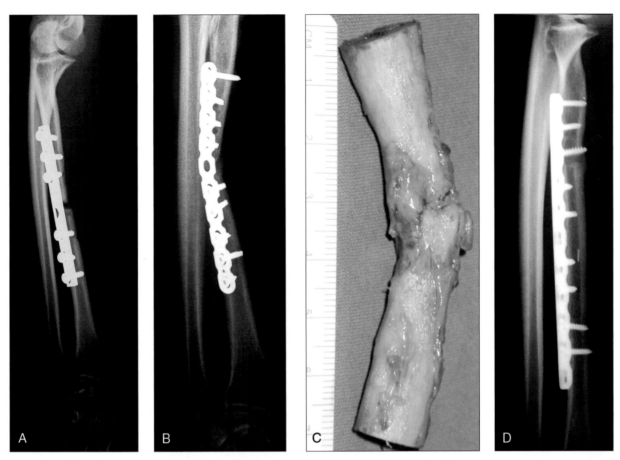

Figure 2   A Gustilo grade II open fracture of the left radius in a 30-year-old man. A noncompression plate was used as the primary treatment. AP radiographs demonstrate the nonunion (**A**), which probably resulted from a poor reduction of the fracture and insufficient stability of the implant, and the subsequent attempt at cancellous bone graft from the iliac crest (**B**), which was not successful due to the poorly vascularized recipient bed and inadequate plate selection. **C**, Photograph of the 7 cm of fibrous tissue and sclerotic bone that were resected at final revision to reach healthy tissue. The defect was reconstructed by means of a vascularized fibula graft fixed by a long low-contact bridging plate. **D**, AP radiograph shows the bone union achieved after 6 months.

Case Management and Outcome

The left radius was exposed using the Henry approach and the plate was removed. The nonunion site was observed to be invaded by fibrous tissue and a residual portion of the previously attempted bone graft. The bone appeared to be improperly vascularized in the diaphyseal segments on both sides of the pseudarthrosis for an extension of 7 cm (**Figure 2**, C). At wrist level, the radial epiphysis had migrated proximally about 2 cm and subsequently had aligned incorrectly with the caput ulnae, so the final length of the fibula graft had to be about 9 cm to restore the physiologic radial length. The bone fixation by LCP resulted in fusion of the graft with the host bone within 6 months (**Figure 2**, *D*).

Minimal functional impairment was observed in the elbow and radiocarpal joints at 8-month follow-up, although a slight limitation of supination remained as a residual deficit.

CASE 3: OPEN FRACTURE OF BOTH BONES OF THE FOREARM (SMALL GAP)

History

A 45-year-old man sustained a severe crush injury to the right arm, resulting in a Gustilo grade IIIC fracture of the radius and ulna. Within 5 hours of the initial injury, blood supply to the hand was restored with a vein graft, the wounds were débrided, and the fractures were fixed. The wrist fracture healed, but the radius and ulna both developed nonunions. Eight months later, autologous corticocancellous bone grafts and new compression plates were applied to both forearm bones.

Current Problem

Although bone grafting and plating were performed properly, the distal portion of the graft on the ulna did not heal, resulting in an atrophic nonunion with a gap of about 1 cm (Figure 3, A). The patient reported pain in the forearm as well as functional impairment. Persistence of inadequately vascularized recipient bone likely was the reason for the nonunion.

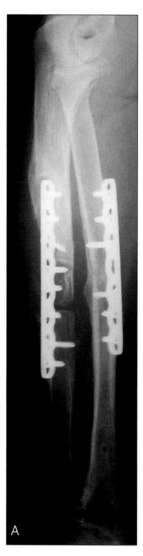

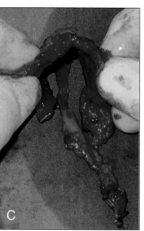
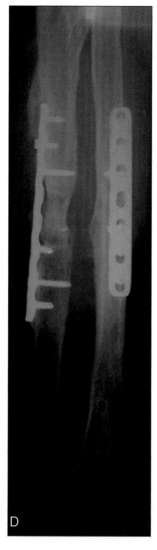

Figure 3 A nonunion of the radius and ulna after a grade IIIC open fracture of the forearm. Cortico-cancellous bone autografts were used to treat the nonunion. The procedure was successful in the radius, but in the ulna only the proximal aspect of the graft united with the recipient bone. **A,** AP radiograph demonstrates the atrophic pseudarthrosis that recurred within 1 year. **B,** Photograph of the vascularized corticoperiosteal flap from the medial condyle of the femur, which was suggested by the small size of the defect, the stability of the implant, and the need for vascularized tissue with a high osteogenetic potential. **C,** Properly manipulated, the flap may be pliable and suitable to be wrapped around the defect. **D,** AP radiograph demonstrates the bone fusion that was achieved within 3 months of the flap. No modification was made to the implants; the bone healing is due to the biologic impulse of the flap.

Although the size of the bone defect precluded the use of a vascularized fibula graft, a new cancellous bone graft was unlikely to be successful due to the poorly vascularized fracture environment.

Case Management and Outcome

Even small gaps may be difficult to treat with conventional techniques. In this case, a corticocancellous bone graft was not successful, even though it had been properly fixed with a compression plate. Nonunion and mild resorption occurred at the distal junction of the graft, suggesting an insufficient blood supply in the recipient bone, which required vascularized tissue to heal. The small size of the defect discouraged the use of a vascularized fibula graft in favor of a less invasive procedure. An osteoperiosteal graft from the medial condyle of the femur was chosen.

A 5-cm x 3-cm bone flap was harvested based on the articular branch of the descending genicular artery, including the periosteum, the cortex, and a thin layer of cancellous bone (**Figure 3,** *B*). Parallel cuts that interrupted the cortex and spared the periosteum were made to render the graft pliable and suitable to be wrapped around the bone defect (**Figure 3,** *C*).

At the recipient site, the nonunion was cleared of fibrous and scarred tissue and the gap was filled with cancellous bone chips from the femoral condyle. The plate appeared to be quite stable and was left in place. The periosteal flap was wrapped around the defect and the plate and then sutured to itself. Microvascular anastomoses were performed end to end to a superficial vein and the common interosseous artery.

Range-of-motion exercises were started immediately after surgery and the bone was checked radiographically every month. A complete fusion of the graft was observed 3 months postoperatively (**Figure 3,** *D*).

CASE 4: COMMINUTED OPEN FRACTURE OF THE WRIST
History

A 42-year-old man sustained a gunshot wound to the wrist, at close range. The resulting comminuted

Gustilo IIIB wrist fracture was complicated by contaminated wounds affecting both the volar and dorsal aspects of the distal forearm and multiple tendon lacerations. The ulnar and median nerves were spared. During emergency surgery, the wound was débrided, fragments of bullet were removed, and the fractures were temporarily fixed with Kirschner wires.

Current Problem

Three weeks after surgery, the patient presented with severe local infection, massive bone loss at the radiocarpal level, extensor tendon defects, and a dehiscence of the dorsal wound. Attempts to reconstruct the joint were impaired by infection and bone loss. A reasonable reconstruction plan had to include eradication of the infection, reconstruction of the large bony defect, tendon repair, and soft-tissue coverage.

Case Management and Outcome

After secondary débridement of the wound, the resulting bony defect involved the entire distal radial epiphysis. Loss of soft tissue involved the extensor tendons and dorsal skin. An antibiotic-impregnated cement spacer was implanted to fill the dead space at the radiocarpal level (**Figure 4,** *A*), and the extensor tendon stumps were marked for secondary reconstruction. The wrist was stabilized with an external fixator.

After 3 months, in the absence of any signs of infection, final reconstruction with an osteocutaneous fibula flap was planned (**Figure 4,** *B*). A 12-cm-long graft was used to reconstruct the final defect of the radius and bypass the carpus to reach the base of the third metacarpal bone and achieve a total wrist fusion. A longitudinal slot was carved in the scaphoid and capitate to improve the lodging of the fibula. A bridging LCP was then used to stabilize the bones. The injured extensor tendons were grafted and covered by the skin paddle that had been harvested with the fibula.

Radiographs taken 7 months after surgery demonstrated stable bony union (**Figure 4,** *C*). Reliable skin coverage and the restoration of finger range of motion were achieved at 3 months postoperatively (**Figure 4,** *D*).

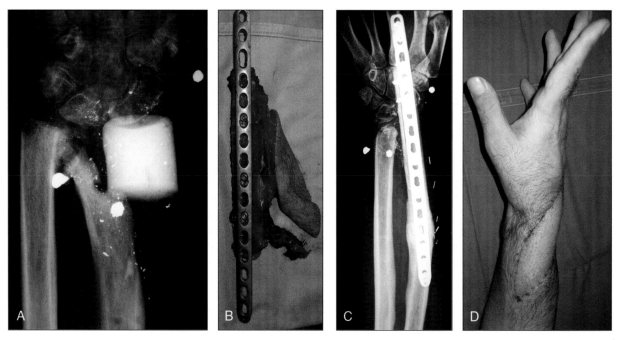

Figure 4 A 42-year-old manual worker sustained a gunshot wound to the right wrist, at close range. **A,** AP radiograph demonstrates the antibiotic-impregnated cement spacer used to fill the dead space. The spacer remained in place for 3 months, and the wrist was stabilized by means of an external fixator. **B,** Photograph of the osteocutaneous fibula flap used to achieve a stable wrist fusion. **C,** AP radiograph taken 7 months after surgery demonstrates no recurrence of infection and healed bone at both junctions. **D,** Clinical photograph shows the acceptable cosmetic and functional results that were achieved 10 months after surgery.

DISCUSSION
Planning the Reconstruction

Conventional options for treating bone defects include corticocancellous bone graft from the iliac crest, autologous nonvascularized fibula graft, allograft, and bone transportation techniques, but none of these techniques should be used for large bone gaps resulting from open fractures. Nonvascularized autografts should be used only for small defects because they produce unpredictable results in larger defects.[1-3] They also are contraindicated in infected, scarred, and poorly vascularized beds. Massive frozen allografts are primarily used in tumor cases.[4-6] They heal by creeping substitution at the junction between allograft and host bone so a very stable osteosynthesis is mandatory, and prolonged immobilization is recommended. Even when consolidation is achieved, most of the allogenic bone remains totally avascular and prone to stress fractures that are not likely to heal. Finally, bone transportation techniques, such as distraction osteogenesis, have few indications in the upper limb because the devices are uncomfortable, difficult to apply, and pose a risk of neurovascular injury.[7,8] In most open fractures of the upper limb, the size of the defect, the soft-tissue involvement, and the bacterial contamination of the wound strongly suggest the use of vascularized bone grafts.

Free Vascularized Fibula Graft

This option takes advantage of the tubular structure of the fibula, which meets all the biomechanical requirements of the recipient bone. The size of the fibula permits it to fit perfectly in forearm reconstruction, and it also may be used in diaphyseal reconstruction of the humerus.[9-15] In fact, because it is a vascularized bone, the fibula can respond to increased functional demands and undergo hypertrophy of the cortex, eventually achieving the same diameter as the host bone. The typical indication for vascularized fibula transfer in upper limb skeletal reconstruction is to bridge a gap longer than 6 cm. Gaps of this size are not uncommon because, in current clinical practice, it is usually necessary to perform a very aggressive débridement of the bone to remove all of the nonvascularized and potentially infected tissue. This débridement leads to a significant gap—usually much longer than the actual defect before débridement—and it may be properly reconstructed by means of a vascularized fibula transfer.

Osteocutaneous Fibula Flap

In most individuals, at least three cutaneous perforators originate from the peroneal vascular bundle in the distal two thirds of the leg. These vessels are located in the posterior crural septum of the lateral compartment and pierce the fascia to supply the lateral skin of the leg. A skin paddle as large as 32 cm x 10 cm can be harvested with the bone, providing a reliable osteocutaneous flap. The osteocutaneous fibula flap can be very useful, particularly in dealing with distal forearm reconstruction.[16] At this level, severe open fractures are more often complicated by soft-tissue damage with exposure of tendons, nerves, and vessels. Simultaneous reconstruction of bone and skin may be achieved in a one-stage surgery, providing excellent coverage to deep structures.

Free Osteoperiosteal Flap

In 1988, Masquelet and associates[17] described a pedicled reverse-flow osteoperiosteal flap from the distal femur. Six years later, Doi and Sakai[18] described a free corticoperiosteal flap from the medial condyle of the femur used for the treatment of bony defects of the forearm and metacarpal bones. The periosteum of the medial condyle is supplied by two vascular sources: the superomedial genicular vessels and the descending genicular vessels. Both arise from the superficial femoral artery, but the latter usually are preferred because of their length and dimension. The periosteum is quite thin and fragile in adults, so the underlying cortical bone also must be harvested. This technique provides a more consistent graft and preserves the cambium layer of the periosteum, which is of paramount importance for new bone formation. The free corticoperiosteal flap is thin, pliable, and well vascularized and has intrinsic bone-forming potential, making it an ideal reconstructive option for recalcitrant nonunion with a small gap in the clavicle and the bones of the upper limb, including the scaphoid.[19]

Management of Infection

For severe bacterial contamination following a recent injury, aggressive débridement should be performed as soon as possible. The procedure includes a wide-margin resection of the infected and poorly vascularized tissues. When a large residual gap is present, beads of antibiotic-impregnated cement should be placed in the dead space, an external fixator applied, and temporary closure of the skin achieved. For massive soft-tissue defects, vacuum-assisted closure (VAC) therapy may be used to drain and keep the wound clean. Final reconstruction should be performed as soon as the risk of infection subsides.

In long-standing osteomyelitis, the extent of the medullary involvement of the bone should be assessed with MRI preoperatively. All infected and nonvascularized bone must be resected according to the principles of oncologic surgery. If resection appears to have successfully eradicated the infected tissue, immediate reconstruction with vascularized bone transfer may be performed. Conversely, in very severe cases, a custom-made antibiotic-impregnated cement spacer should be used to fill the gap and should be maintained for 3 months. After this period, the spacer can be removed and replaced with a vascularized fibula graft.

Osteosynthesis

In the authors' experience, rigid and stable osteosynthesis is a key indicator for the success of the procedure. The consolidation time of a vascularized graft is still longer than that of an equivalent bifocal fracture. A reliable bone fixation is therefore mandatory before beginning an early rehabilitation program and to improve the functional outcome. No secondary fracture was observed in our series of patients, thus confirming that stable osteosynthesis can prevent this complication.

The host-donor bone junction should be properly managed to improve the healing process.[20] In the humerus, the size of the fibula allows for an intramedullary location of the graft at both contact points with the bone that is grafted with the fibula, and we recommend overlapping the junction with a redundant flap of fibular periosteum. Although a step-cut osteotomy is demanding and carries a risk of malrotation, we strongly suggest using this procedure whenever possible for forearm reconstruction because it increases the contact between the bones and provides a more stable bone fixation.

The new-generation LCP plates are very reliable implants that are fixed with unicortical screws. Such plates make it possible to achieve compression at the osteotomy sites using traditional bicortical screws and are less invasive to the fibula than stabilization with unicortical screws.

The humerus is exposed to significant torque stress, so it is advisable to use a single long plate that bypasses the intercalary fibula rather than two short plates that can leave a weak point in the midportion of the fibular shaft. Although the forearm is a two-bone segment and therefore highly resistant to mechanical stress, it is desirable to use a single bridging plate with compression at both sides when reconstructing the radius and ulna.

When performing total wrist fusion by free vascularized fibula graft, we suggest carving a longitudinal slot in the carpal bones coaxial with the third metacarpal bone. The depth of the slot should be equal to the transverse diameter of the fibula, the distal tip of which should make perfect contact with the base of the third metacarpal bone. This arrangement optimizes the contact of the distal portion of the graft with the dorsal aspect of the carpal bones and reduces the dorsal bulging of the bone and of the plate, which may cause tension during skin closure.

STRATEGIES FOR MINIMIZING COMMON COMPLICATIONS

Key strategies for minimizing the complications of vascularized bone grafting include careful preoperative planning, harvesting adequate skin to compensate for the difficulty in closing wounds enlarged by swelling, planning for vascular inflow and outflow,

and vigilant management of the donor site. Vascular reconstruction includes the liberal use of interposition vein grafts, where necessary. Strategies are designed to provide vascular inflow. The anastomoses should not be exposed and should not be under tension. In humeral reconstruction, the radial artery, vena commitantes, and cephalic vein have been used as inflow and outflow conduits. Harvesting the radial artery distally at the level of the wrist and turning it proximally to provide vascular inflow for humeral reconstructions is often advantageous. By taking the entire length of the fibula, additional vascular pedicle length can be dissected off the fibula.

Strategies for preventing bone loss following open fractures relate to radical débridement and a second-look procedure after the initial débridement. Expeditious coverage of open fractures and appropriate use of antibiotics can prevent subsequent infection and ultimate bone loss from osteomyelitis. Such measures are ultimately designed to preclude the need for vascularized bone grafting.

REFERENCES

1. Stevenson S, Emery SE, Goldberg VM: Factors affecting bone graft incorporation. *Clin Orthop Relat Res* 1996;324:66-74.
2. Khan SN, Cammisa FP Jr, Sandhu HS, Diwan AD, Girardi FP, Lane JM: The biology of bone grafting. *J Am Acad Orthop Surg* 2005;13(1):77-86.
3. Rtaimate M, Laffargue P, Farez E, Larivière J, Baranzelli MC: Reconstruction of the distal radius for primary bone tumors using a non-vascularized fibular graft (report of 4 cases). *Chir Main* 2001;20(4):272-279.
4. Mankin HJ, Gebhardt MC, Jennings LC, Springfield DS, Tomford WW: Long-term results of allograft replacement in the management of bone tumors. *Clin Orthop Relat Res* 1996;324:86-97.
5. Kocher MS, Gebhardt MC, Mankin HJ: Reconstruction of the distal aspect of the radius with the use of an osteoarticular allograft after excision of a skeletal tumor. *J Bone J Surg* 1998;80:407-419.
6. Hornicek FJ, Gebhardt MC, Tomford WW, et al: Factors affecting nonunion of the allograft-host junction. *Clin Orthop Relat Res* 2001;382:87-98.
7. Esser RD: Treatment of a bone defect of the forearm by bone transport. A case report. *Clin Orthop Relat Res* 1996;326:221-224.

8. Villa A, Paley D, Catagni MA, Bell D, Cattaneo R: Lengthening of the forearm by the Ilizarov technique. *Clin Orthop Relat Res* 1990;250:125-137.

9. Taylor GI, Miller GD, Ham FJ: The free vascularized bone graft. A clinical extension of microvascular techniques. *Plast Reconstr Surg* 1975;55(5):533-544.

10. Olekas J, Guobys A: Vascularised bone transfer for defects and pseudarthroses of forearm bones. *J Hand Surg Br* 1991;16(4):406-408.

11. Mattar Júnior J, Azze RJ, Ferreira MC, Starck R, Canedo AC: Vascularized fibular graft for management of severe osteomyelitis of the upper extremity. *Microsurgery* 1994;15(1):22-27.

12. Yajima H, Tamai S, Ono H, Kizaki K, Yamauchi T: Free vascularized fibula grafts in surgery of the upper limb. *J Reconstr Microsurg* 1999;15(7):515-521.

13. Stevanovic M, Gutow AP, Sharpe F: The management of bone defects of the forearm after trauma. *Hand Clin* 1999;15(2):299-318.

14. Adani R, Delcroix L, Innocenti M, et al: Reconstruction of large posttraumatic skeletal defects of the forearm by vascularized free fibular graft. *Microsurgery* 2004;24(6):423-429.

15. del Piñal F, Innocenti M: Evolving concepts in the management of the bone gap in the upper limb. Long and small defects. *J Plast Reconstr Aesthet Surg* 2007;60(7):776-792.

16. Jupiter JB, Gerhard HJ, Guerrero JA, Nunley JA, Levin LS: Treatment of segmental defects of the radius with use of the vascularized osteoseptocutaneous fibular autogenous graft. *J Bone Joint Surg Am* 1997;79(4):542-550.

17. Masquelet AC, Romana MC, Penteado CV, Carlioz H: Vascularized periosteal grafts. Anatomic description, experimental study, preliminary report of clinical experience. *Rev Chir Orthop Reparatrice Appar Mot* 1988;74(Suppl 2):240-243.

18. Doi K, Sakai K: Vascularized periosteal bone graft from the supracondylar region of the femur. *Microsurgery* 1994;15(5):305-315.

19. Doi K, Oda T, Soo-Heong T, Nanda V: Free vascularized bone graft for nonunion of the scaphoid. *J Hand Surg Am* 2000;25(3):507-519.

20. Heitmann C, Erdmann D, Levin LS: Treatment of segmental defects of the humerus with an osteoseptocutaneous fibular transplant. *J Bone Joint Surg Am* 2002;84-A(12):2216-2223.

Chapter 2

COMMON DECISION-MAKING ERRORS IN LIMB SALVAGE

Andrew N. Pollak, MD

CASE PRESENTATION

History

A 45-year-old man sustained a mangled right leg in a motorcycle accident. His motorcycle had swerved off the road and struck a guardrail, resulting in injury to his leg and causing him to be ejected from the motorcycle and thrown approximately 40 feet into an area containing trees and brush. The patient initially was taken by ground ambulance to a local trauma center, where he was evaluated. The patient was advised that amputation of the right leg was necessary because he had an insensate foot, severe soft-tissue and bony injuries, and a history of diabetes. At his request, the patient was transferred to my center for an opinion about the feasibility and advisability of limb salvage.

Current Problem and Treatment

The patient arrived approximately 6 hours after the initial injury. Upon examination, the patient was awake and alert but anxious. Some of the anxiety appeared to be related to the obvious limb-threatening lower extremity injury. His heart rate and blood pressure were 110 and 100/70, respectively. Initial trauma evaluation, including a CT scan of the chest, abdomen, and pelvis, was repeated. The evaluation confirmed that the injury to the leg was isolated but revealed evidence of underresuscitation, including a serum lactate value of 5.2 mmol/dl and a hematocrit of 24% (despite underresuscitation). In retrospect, the patient's initial anxiety likely was related partially to

Dr. Pollak or an immediate family member serves as a board member, owner, officer, or committee member of the Orthopaedic Trauma Association; is a member of a speakers' bureau or has made paid presentations on behalf of KCI and Smith & Nephew; serves as a paid consultant to or is an employee of Smith & Nephew and Extra-Ortho; and has received research or institutional support from AO, KCI, Smith & Nephew, Stryker, Synthes, Wyeth, and Zimmer.

ongoing hypovolemic shock, as demonstrated by the significantly elevated serum lactate levels. Antibiotics, including a first-generation cephalosporin and an aminoglycoside, had been administered at the initial hospital on presentation and were repeated at my center 6 hours later.

My trauma team and I reviewed the findings, including the radiographs (**Figure 1**, *A* and *B*), with the patient. We explained that, in our opinion, the lack of plantar sensation did not represent an indication for early amputation. We recommended that, despite the obvious severity of the limb injury, surgical débridement and stabilization be delayed temporarily pending further fluid resuscitation. We also noted that it would be difficult to make a well-informed decision about long-term salvage in such a complex situation at this time, given the acute trauma and ongoing resuscitation. Therefore, we decided that proceeding with initial limb salvage did not appear contraindicated as long as we were able to achieve adequate resolution of physiologic stability through fluid replenishment (including blood replacement). Initial limb salvage procedures would give the patient time to understand the complexity of the problem and consult with friends and family before making a final decision about amputation or limb salvage.

The patient and his family agreed. Resuscitation was achieved, and, 12 hours after the injury, the patient was taken to the operating room, where a thorough débridement of the injury—a massive medial soft-tissue defect and a smaller lateral soft-tissue defect—was performed. At the time of surgical débridement, we confirmed that a soft-tissue flap would be necessary to achieve wound coverage and that free-tissue transfer was more desirable than a rotational flap because of the size of the defect, its location, and the underlying high-energy fracture pattern. Marked débridement of bone was necessary because of the devitalization of fragments. A thorough inspection of the soft-tissue injury revealed that the tibial nerve remained intact through the zone of injury, suggesting that potential for recovery of function existed. External fixation was selected as the initial tool for skeletal stabilization because it facilitated repeat surgical débridement. It also allowed for amputation in the event the patient changed his mind at a later date. We

managed the open wound initially with negative pressure therapy to enhance wound drainage while maintaining a closed environment that would prevent repeated exposure of the wound to the bacterial populations of the hospital.

Approximately 36 hours after the initial procedure, we took the patient back to the operating room for a planned, staged repeat surgical débridement. At that time, significantly more muscle tissue appeared devitalized and required débridement. Further discussion with the patient led to a decision to proceed with limb salvage despite the obvious severity of the injury and the underlying diabetes. Approximately 48 hours later, another planned, staged surgical débridement revealed minimal additional tissue devitalization and a massive but relatively healthy-appearing soft-tissue defect (**Figure 1**, *C*). One day later, our plastic surgical team performed free-tissue transfer to cover the medial wound and a combination of delayed primary closure plus split-thickness skin graft was used to cover the lateral side. An intramedullary nail was inserted and the external fixator was revised during the same surgery. We elected to keep a modified version of the external fixator frame in place around the nail for 4 weeks to prevent ankle equinus without using a splint that would cover the flap and to facilitate limb elevation during initial flap healing.

After 4 weeks, the frame was removed. The underlying bony defect consisted of a large anterior wedge defect with residual posterior bony point contact (**Figure 1**, *D* and *E*). The timing of the definitive internal fixation procedure and the flap was coordinated carefully. Our goal was to place the tibial nail at the same time that we performed the wound coverage procedure, to avoid exposing the final implant to contamination during an additional surgical procedure. We also sought to achieve definitive internal fixation and flap coverage as rapidly as safely possible after initial injury to minimize the risk of infection.

Flap healing was delayed markedly, and several complications developed. First, although the initial free flap survived, a split-thickness skin graft used to cover a portion of the wound that did not require free-tissue transfer completely sloughed off. This area was treated with local wound care, and good soft-tissue healing eventually resulted. During the subsequent 5 months, several superficial infectious

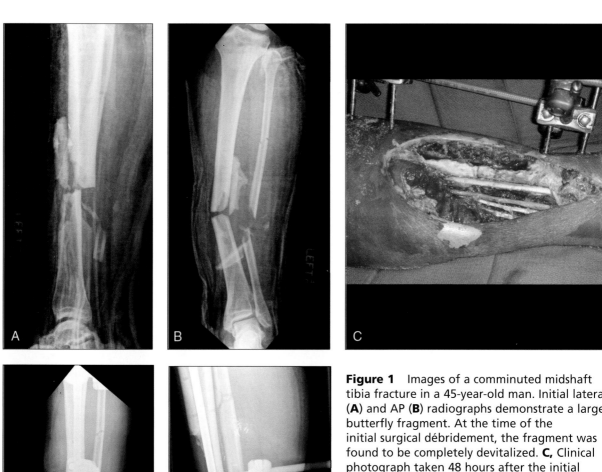

Figure 1 Images of a comminuted midshaft tibia fracture in a 45-year-old man. Initial lateral (**A**) and AP (**B**) radiographs demonstrate a large butterfly fragment. At the time of the initial surgical débridement, the fragment was found to be completely devitalized. **C,** Clinical photograph taken 48 hours after the initial wound débridement demonstrates that the residual tissues appear viable and clean. Free-tissue transfer was used shortly thereafter to achieve wound coverage medially, with the lateral side closed using a combination of delayed primary closure and split-thickness skin grafting. AP (**D**) and lateral (**E**) radiographs demonstrate the intramedullary nail used for definitive internal fixation. The external fixator was modified after the nail and flap were placed. It was used for approximately 4 weeks in conjunction with the nail to provide stabilization of the ankle and to facilitate elevation of the leg.

processes developed, including small abscesses apparently related to suture reactions and episodes of superficial cellulitis. To prevent the development of severe disuse osteopenia and to encourage proprioceptive feedback, weight bearing was permitted during this time. After all of the infectious events resolved (inflammatory markers, including white blood cell count, erythrocyte sedimentation rate, and C-reactive protein levels, were all within normal limits, suggesting that no ongoing infection was present), repeat radiographics were obtained. They demonstrated persistence of the major bone defect and nonunion in the region of bone-to-bone contact, but overall good maintenance of alignment.

DISCUSSION
Recognizing the Problem and High-Risk Situations

The treatment of high-energy lower extremity trauma often requires the surgeon to help the patient make a series of informed decisions about the best course of treatment given the patient's particular situation. Decision-making errors regarding limb salvage are most likely to occur when surgeons use dogmatic approaches to treatment. Care must be taken at all times to individualize treatment according to each patient's expectations, needs, and overall psychosocial support structure. Several pitfalls exist in the management of limb-threatening lower extremity trauma. Such pitfalls include considering the absence of plantar sensation as an indication for amputation, overreliance on lower extremity salvage scores, inadequate débridement of open fractures, flap selection issues, and factors relating to the patient's medical status.

Reliance on Plantar Sensation

The presence or absence of plantar sensation often has been cited as an indication for limb salvage or amputation, respectively, following high-energy, limb-threatening lower extremity trauma. At least one important study has pointed to anatomic discontinuity in the tibial nerve as representing an absolute indication for amputation.

In 1985, Lange and associates[1] published a retrospective review of 23 cases of type IIIC open tibia fractures that were followed for at least 1 year. Fourteen of the 23 underwent amputation, 5 of which were performed during the initial hospitalization and 9 after discharge. Five of the 9 patients who underwent limb salvage procedures experienced significant long-term problems. After reviewing the failed salvage procedures and delayed amputations, the authors expressed the opinion that

anatomic disruption of the tibial nerve represented an absolute indication for amputation.

In 2002, the Lower Extremity Assessment Project (LEAP) study was published. The LEAP study was a prospective, observational comparison of amputation to limb salvage in 601 high-energy lower extremity injuries treated at eight level 1 trauma centers.[2]

Factors that surgeons described as important in the decision-making process included the severity of the bony or soft-tissue injury and the presence or absence of vascular injury. Most interestingly, however, they also described the presence or absence of plantar sensation as an important determining factor in their treatment decision. Plantar sensation was used as a proxy for the anatomic continuity of the tibial nerve.

The problem with using plantar sensation as a proxy for the assessment of anatomic continuity is that other factors associated with the acute injury, such as ischemic and neuropraxic injuries to the nerves, which may be temporary, can contribute to the lack of plantar sensation. In many cases, the nature of the open injury prevents a direct inspection of the tibial nerve throughout the zone of injury, making it difficult to determine whether the nerve is in fact anatomically intact. It is even more difficult to accurately determine whether the nerve will recover over time if it is anatomically intact but dysfunctional at the time of the initial examination.

For all these reasons, using plantar sensation as a proxy for the continuity of the tibial nerve may be invalid. Furthermore, the only support in the literature for using tibial nerve continuity as an indication for salvage versus amputation is the retrospective study by Lange and associates.[1] Other clinical scenarios in which plantar sensation is absent do not call for amputation necessarily. Such scenarios include open tibial fracture associated with spinal cord injury or diabetes. In these cases—even in the absence of plantar sensation—limb salvage often is undertaken; for example, in the case of an open tibial shaft fracture in a patient with associated complete spinal cord injury.

In 2005, Bosse and associates[2] mined the LEAP data to determine whether the presence or absence of plantar sensation, as determined at the time of initial examination in the emergency department, represented a predictor of ultimate limb salvage.

The most interesting finding of this study was that no significant difference existed in the presence or absence of plantar sensation at the time of final follow-up between patients in the control group, who presented initially with sensate feet, and those in the salvage group, who presented initially with insensate feet. A similar percentage of patients in the control group were insensate 24 months after injury as in the salvage group. These findings indicate that the presence or absence of initial plantar sensation is an extremely poor predictor of the presence or absence of plantar sensation at 2 years after high-energy injury. Thus, despite being one of the most important variables listed by surgeons in their decisions about whether to amputate or salvage a severely injured lower extremity, the presence or absence of plantar sensation actually is a very poor indicator of ultimate tibial nerve function and likely is not a good proxy for anatomic continuity of the tibial nerve. This study strongly suggests that presence or absence of plantar sensation at the time of initial presentation should not be used as a determining factor in deciding whether to proceed with amputation of a mangled lower extremity.

Utility of Lower Extremity Salvage Scores

At least five separate scoring systems have been developed to assess injury severity after high-energy lower extremity trauma.[3-7] Bosse and associates[8] evaluated these systems in the context of the LEAP study to assess their ability to predict the need for amputation, the likelihood of achieving limb salvage, and the ultimate outcome. Low scores on all scoring systems were found to be good predictors of successful limb salvage overall. The converse, however, did not hold true: high scores were poor predictors of the need for amputation. None of the scoring systems was able to predict whether a limb would be permanently dysfunctional, based on the components of the injury or any other objectively measurable criterion. Because the scores were developed primarily to help surgeons decide when a limb should be amputated, these results are terribly disappointing.

Ly and associates[9] used the LEAP database to evaluate the relationship between initial salvage scores and long-term functional outcome. They found no correlation between the score on any of the five published lower extremity injury severity scales and functional outcome at 6 or 24 months after injury. Predicting patient satisfaction after high-energy lower extremity trauma also is difficult. Measurable characteristics of the patient, the injury, and the treatment of that injury seem to be less important than factors related to physical function, depression, and return-to-work in predicting self-reported patient satisfaction after injury.[10]

Débridement of Open Fractures

Another common error in the initial management of open fractures is inadequate débridement. Anecdotal evidence suggests that inadequate débridement of severe lower extremity injury often is not only a cause of infection but also the ultimate cause of the need for amputation following such injuries.

Dead tissue serves as a nidus for infection and provides no functional benefit in the context of the mangled extremity. There is no reason, therefore, to fail to débride all obviously dead tissue in a severe open injury. Unfortunately, some treating surgeons are unfamiliar with the criteria for assessing tissue viability in the early phases after injury, and some of these criteria have not been validated scientifically. Finally, surgeons who are unfamiliar with the regular débridement of open fractures often are reluctant to débride tissue that has uncertain viability at the time of initial inspection.

Determining tissue viability at the time of initial wound inspection includes an assessment of color, consistency, contractility, and capacity to bleed. The number of criteria that need to be met before tissue should be declared definitively nonviable is not at all clear. Studies examining the use of these factors in determining absolute tissue viability have been largely subjective. These multiple variables suggest that no good substitute currently exists for experience when making decisions about what tissue to salvage and what tissue to débride (up to and including the ultimate débridement procedure, amputation).

Because an open fracture often is considered an emergency and the débridement is performed urgently, sometimes in the middle of the night, an experienced surgeon may not be available to assess tissue viability. The rationale behind declaring open fractures an emergency, however, is based on poorly substantiated recommendations from studies performed before the modern era of antibiotic administration. One example is Gustilo and Anderson's[11] 1973 review of 1,171 open fractures, in which they stated—without a specific reference—that urgent surgical débridement was mandatory following open fracture. The doubling times for bacteria in culture were used to support the additional recommendation that débridement should be accomplished within 6 hours of injury whenever possible.[12]

The LEAP study data were analyzed to assess the validity of the assumption that early débridement of open fractures leads to decreased rates of infection.[13] The authors reviewed 315 open fractures in the LEAP study population and demonstrated that the time from injury to admission to the definitive treatment center was an independent predictor of infection risk, but that neither the time from injury to surgical débridement nor the time from admission to surgical débridement was a significant predictor. Other authors also have demonstrated that the time from injury to débridement of the open fracture is not an important predictor of infection risk following open fracture.[14-16] Webb and associates[17] suggested that the timing of débridement also fails to predict outcome. Taken collectively, these data suggest that delaying surgical stabilization is warranted if it is necessary to accommodate the availability of an experienced surgeon. Stated differently, no support exists in the literature for treating these injuries emergently when qualified surgeons who have significant experience in assessing tissue viability and performing surgical débridement are unavailable.

Flap Selection in Soft-Tissue Coverage Procedures

Free-tissue transfer has been used successfully in the management of high-energy lower extremity injuries with major soft-tissue defects.[18] Other options include rotational flaps, fasciocutaneous flaps, and local methods of promoting granulation tissue coverage (such as negative pressure wound therapy).[19] Free-tissue transfer is the most versatile tool available for covering large defects, but it also remains the most technically demanding option and often is considered to be associated with the highest rate of complications. Rotational flaps are technically less challenging than is free-tissue transfer, are sufficiently versatile to meet the demands of many different injuries, and are thought to be associated with fewer complications. The disadvantage of rotational flaps is that the tissue is taken from an area proximate to the zone of injury and therefore may be compromised, thereby increasing the risk of complication and failure.

In their analysis of complications after limb salvage in the overall management of a group of severe, type III open fractures, Georgiadis and associates[20] reported flap loss in 34%, need for flap elevation in 41%, and initial free-flap failure in 90%. Using the LEAP population, rates of flap success and failure were evaluated while controlling for potentially confounding variables related to patient characteristics, injury characteristics, and treatment characteristics.[21] In reviewing 195 limbs from the LEAP study with open fractures that required flap coverage and were available for at least 6 months of available follow-up, complications were noted to have occurred in 27% of patients, with a 21% rate of wound infection and a 5% incidence of frank wound necrosis. Overall, 8% of flaps were lost and surgical treatment of complications was required in 87% of those cases in which a complication was noted to occur. Despite the higher grade of muscle injury noted in the free flap group, no differences in complication rates were noted between the free flap and rotational flap groups in bivariate analysis. In multivariate analysis, however, when comparing patients treated with a rotational flap for an AO type C injury with those treated with a free flap for an AO type A or B injury, the risk of developing a complication was almost six times higher in the rotational flap group. This study suggests that, in the context of a high-energy fracture pattern and a soft-tissue defect requiring flap coverage, the use of free-tissue transfer is associated with fewer complications over the short term.

Another interesting finding from this multivariate model is that the time from injury to wound coverage was not an independent predictor of risk of complication. Previous investigators had suggested that the timing of wound coverage was an important factor.[22,23] Using multivariate modeling and collecting information about a broad spectrum of factors likely to influence the complication rate, it is possible to control for bias that may have been introduced into prior studies. It appears that a better interpretation of some of the earlier data would be that treating surgeons should recognize injury severity and avoid early coverage in situations in which adequate débridement has not yet been achieved.

Patient Factors

Tolerance of Massive Blood Loss

Recent experiences from the military conflicts in Iraq and Afghanistan have highlighted the importance of early and aggressive control of extremity bleeding in lower extremity blast injury.[24] Many of the same lessons likely can be applied to civilian scenarios.

Severe lower extremity trauma can be associated with massive hemorrhage. In addition, attempted limb salvage, particularly in the early phases, often can be associated with massive intraoperative hemorrhage. One absolute contraindication to limb salvage is a patient who is unable to tolerate the extreme blood loss that may be associated with the limb salvage procedure.

One way to avert this problem is to do as much as possible under tourniquet control. Unfortunately, tourniquet-induced ischemia times longer than 2 hours are tolerated poorly at the local tissue level and can result in significant systemic consequences secondary to the reperfusion injury associated with tourniquet release. The challenge therefore is to leave the tourniquet on long enough to control hemorrhage and avoid the physiologic insult of exsanguination but remove it soon enough to avoid the physiologic insult of reperfusion injury. Critical to attaining that balance is the ability to achieve local wound hemostasis during the initial time that the tourniquet is inflated. If the operating surgeon cannot achieve such hemostasis during that time, then early amputation should be considered.

Furthermore, a careful early inspection of the anatomy of the injury is warranted to make sure that the surgeon is not putting the patient at risk of physiologic injury by attempting to salvage a limb that is otherwise unsalvageable anatomically. One such example is the acute transection injury that involves the complete anatomic disruption of all major nervous, arterial, venous, and bony structures. The patient with a near amputation who requires revascularization likely will not benefit from such revascularization and therefore should not be exposed to the potential risks of limb salvage.

Physiologic Instability

The capacity of the patient to tolerate the physiologic insult associated with limb salvage also must be considered when deciding whether to proceed with limb salvage or amputation in the context of multiple trauma. This physiologic insult includes multiple prolonged surgical procedures, local and systemic infection risk, blood loss, and ischemia-reperfusion injury associated with the use of a tourniquet or the reperfusion of an ischemic limb.

Physiologic stability must be assessed thoroughly before proceeding with limb salvage. This assessment should include any associated injuries the patient may have sustained and the patient's medical history. Associated injuries that could contraindicate limb salvage include severe traumatic brain injury with elevated or unstable intracranial pressures. Very little evidence indicates that orthopaedic surgical procedures have a direct adverse impact on intracranial pressure or that they otherwise directly impact associated brain injury detrimentally, but concern exists about the inability to monitor changes in the patient's neurologic condition while the patient is under anesthesia.[25] Furthermore, blood loss associated with a reconstruction procedure may require transfusion of blood products or crystalloid infusion that can produce changes in intracranial pressure. Any unnecessary transport to the operating room of patients with intracranial monitoring devices in place could require the recalibration of the devices, which potentially could result in errors in measuring true intracranial pressures. All of these potential problems put the brain-injured patient at increased risk because of the substantial surgical demand associated with limb salvage.

Severe pulmonary injuries also represent a relative contraindication to major limb salvage surgery.[26] Patients with a reduced capacity to maintain blood oxygenation poorly tolerate the fluid shifts associated with blood loss and subsequent replacement. The risk to the pulmonary capillary membranes in patients with primary lung injuries probably is greater than in patients whose lungs are uninjured.

One of the more common relative contraindications to safe limb salvage surgery is when a patient with a mangled, high-energy lower extremity injury presents with ongoing shock and incomplete resuscitation. The patient's overall level of resuscitation should be assessed carefully before proceeding with limb salvage. Several indications of adequate resuscitation have been used for this purpose. Urine output often is difficult to determine in the first 24 hours after injury and may not always be a good indication of adequate resuscitation. Serum lactate frequently has been used as a proxy for shock and its reversal. If serum lactate levels are normalizing toward 2.0, it is likely safe to proceed with limb reconstruction from the standpoint of shock resolution. If, however, serum lactate levels remain markedly elevated, persistent shock is likely present. This is a significant life-threatening sign. Patients in whom serum lactate does not clear sufficiently within the first 24 hours after injury have a markedly elevated risk of mortality.[27] Limb salvage in these situations obviously is contraindicated.

Patients with comorbidities, such as diabetes or smoking, that increase the risk of complications including nonunion and infection should be counseled about the potential increased risk.

Managing the Problem
Amputation versus Limb Salvage

Caudle and Stern[28] reported a retrospective review of 62 severe open tibia fractures followed for a mean of 2 years. They noted that all of the type IIIC injuries in their series that were treated with salvage eventually resulted in amputation or developed severe chronic complications. They further noted a very high rate of complications in the type IIIB

injuries, particularly in those in which early soft-tissue coverage was not possible. An editorial comment in the *Journal of Bone and Joint Surgery* published concurrently with that study suggested that prolonged salvage procedures should be avoided when "such a course is not indicated."[29] Similarly, Georgiadis and associates[20] reported many more complications in a group of patients with high-grade tibia fractures treated with limb salvage than in those who underwent amputation. The researchers reported an overall 56% incidence of osteomyelitis and a substantial incidence of initial free flap failure.

In the LEAP study, the sickness impact profile (SIP) was used as the principal indicator of health-related quality of life following injury. When comparing the amputation groups with the limb-salvage groups, no differences were seen in associated demographic characteristics. From an injury perspective, those treated with amputation had more severe injuries initially (as would be expected) than those treated with limb salvage. Complications requiring a rehospitalization occurred in more than one third of patients in the study group, and those treated with amputation required rehospitalization less frequently than those treated with reconstruction (again as would be expected).

No significant differences were seen in the SIP scores between the treatment in control groups on direct comparison or in regression analysis, suggesting that no substantial difference was present in measurable outcome between limb salvage and amputation. These findings suggest that the idea of proceeding directly to amputation with the hope of sparing the patient the stress of limb salvage and therefore improving long-term outcome is unfounded.

The data further suggested that complications are likely to develop at some point during the treatment of high-energy lower extremity trauma regardless of the treatment modality selected.

Overall, disability both 2 years and 7 years after high-energy lower extremity trauma remains pronounced. Seven years after injury, 50% of patients still have evidence of substantial disability based on SIP scores, and barely one-third have scores similar to those of their own age and sex who did not sustain severe lower extremity injury.[30]

In examining data that control for patient, injury, and treatment variables in high-energy lower extremity trauma, the only published surgical treatment that has been implicated specifically in poor outcomes is the use of external fixation for definitive stabilization of fractures in limbs with soft-tissue injuries that required muscle flap coverage. Webb and associates[17] demonstrated that overall, limb salvage patients whose fractures were stabilized definitively with external fixators and who required muscle flap coverage had worse results than patients with similarly injured limbs who were treated with internal fixation. Those treated definitively with external fixation that required a muscle flap also had significantly worse outcomes in regression analysis than did those treated with amputation. These data suggest that it would be a mistake to recommend a course of limb salvage over amputation to a patient with a high-energy lower-extremity injury, a fracture requiring definitive treatment with an external fixator, and a soft-tissue defect that requires a muscle flap.

Preventing the Problem
Decision-Making Errors in Limb Salvage

To avoid decision-making errors, careful consideration should be given to a patient's overall condition and individual needs before proceeding with limb salvage. Clearly, no single correct answer applies to every patient regardless of injury severity, surgeon variables, or patient characteristics, including comorbidities. Patients considered for limb salvage should be physiologically fit enough to face the challenges of multiple, prolonged surgical procedures with the potential for major blood loss. Comorbidities may increase the risk of complications and reduce overall success rates. Certain characteristics of an injury may make successful salvage unlikely. To give patients realistic expectations about physical functioning and returning to work, surgeons must advise all patients undergoing reconstruction of high-energy lower extremity trauma early in the process that complications likely will occur and that substantial disability may be permanent. Further research is necessary to help surgeons better understand the most effective treatment regimens for these challenging injuries, but both

anatomic and psychological components of the disease process must be addressed.

A common error in treating patients with limb-threatening high-energy lower extremity trauma is failure of the surgeon to disclose fully the complexity of the injury, the degree of long-term disability likely to be experienced, the likelihood of complications and the overall investment in time and energy necessary for the patient to achieve recovery. Advising patients with limb-threatening lower extremity trauma about the likelihood of complications during their course of treatment and the probable outcomes of treatment is critical to prepare them adequately for the consequences of their injuries. Failure to do so represents a common mistake in limb salvage.

CASE MANAGEMENT AND OUTCOME SUMMARY

For the patient described in the case presentation, whose limb was salvaged but in whom nonunion resulted, our team elected to proceed with treatment of the nonunion by posterolateral bone grafting and fibular plating. We discussed two options at length with the patient: allograft plus recombinant bone morphogenetic protein-2 (rBMP-2) or autograft. Although evidence suggests that allograft plus recombinant rBMP-2 has efficacy similar to that of autograft, such evidence is not robust because the relevant studies have insufficient power. Clinical experience suggests that autogenous posterior iliac crest cancellous graft is the gold standard.

The patient expressed a preference for autograft, so we proceeded with that option, noting that augmentation of the graft material with cancellous allograft might be necessary given the size of the residual bony defect. We used a posterolateral approach to achieve bridging of the fibular defect and long-term stabilization of the limb by creating a synostosis between the tibia and the fibula proximal and distal to the site of nonunion. In approaching the defect posteriorly, we also sought to avoid the tenuous soft-tissue envelope that existed anteriorly.

We also advised the patient that, given the severity of the original injury, the presence of the nonunion, the history of multiple superficial infec-

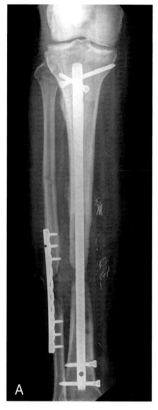
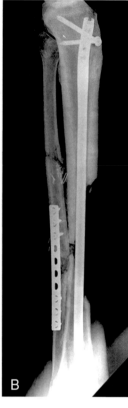

Figure 2 Treatment of the nonunion in the patient shown in Figure 1. AP (**A**) and lateral (**B**) radiographs demonstate a combination of fibular stabilization and grafting plus posterolateral formation of a synostosis between the tibia and fibula using posterior iliac crest cancellous autograft bone plus freeze-dried cancellous allograft bone chips.

tions, and his history of diabetes, our index of suspicion for the presence of an underlying deep infection remained high despite the negative inflammatory markers. Our preoperative plan included obtaining intraoperative frozen section analysis to look for evidence of acute inflammation and intraoperative Gram stain analysis to look for bacteria or white blood cells. If either evaluation increased our suspicion of underlying infection, we planned to abort the graft procedure and await culture results before proceeding.

Intraoperative evaluation revealed healthy-appearing tissue at the nonunion location without any significant fluid collection or purulent material.

Neither frozen section nor Gram stain analysis revealed evidence of acute inflammation. We therefore proceeded with the harvest of the ipsilateral posterior iliac crest for the graft, augmentation of graft volume using cancellous allograft freeze-dried chips, plate stabilization of the segmental fibular defect, and bone grafting to bridge the fibular nonunion and to create a synostosis between the tibia and fibula to achieve long-term stabilization of the leg (**Figure 2**).

Three days after surgery, cultures of the leg grew a few colonies of a sensitive species of *Pseudomonas aeruginosa*. After a consultation with infectious disease specialists and the patient, we elected to treat the infection with 6 weeks of dual antibiotic therapy followed by suppressive doses until the hardware could be removed safely at some point in the distant future.

STRATEGIES FOR MINIMIZING COMMON COMPLICATIONS

Common errors leading to complication have been mentioned previously but warrant repeating. All dead, devitalized, and contaminated tissue must be débrided from open fracture wounds. Failure to do so increases infection risk dramatically. Surgeons must not rely on presenting plantar sensation as a proxy for distal nerve integrity, and must remember that no scoring system alone reliably can define which limbs can be salvaged and which cannot.

Perhaps most important when undertaking limb salvage, patients and surgeons must accept that complications are likely to occur. Patients should be able to feel confident that their surgeon will be vigilant in diagnosing complications early and that he or she will work with them to achieve resolution of the complication and realize the best possible outcome.

REFERENCES

1.   Lange RH, Bach AW, Hansen ST Jr, Johansen KH: Open tibial fractures with associated vascular injuries: Prognosis for limb salvage. *J Trauma* 1985;25(3): 203-208.

2. Bosse MJ, MacKenzie EJ, Kellam JF, et al: An analysis of outcomes of reconstruction or amputation after leg-threatening injuries. *N Engl J Med* 2002;347(24):1924-1931.

3. Helfet DL, Howey T, Sanders R, Johansen K: Limb salvage versus amputation: Preliminary results of the Mangled Extremity Severity Score. *Clin Orthop Relat Res* 1990;256:80-86.

4. Howe HR Jr, Poole GV Jr, Hansen KJ Jr, et al: Salvage of lower extremities following combined orthopedic and vascular trauma: A predictive salvage index. *Am Surg* 1987;53(4):205-208.

5. McNamara MG, Heckman JD, Corley FG: Severe open fractures of the lower extremity: A retrospective evaluation of the Mangled Extremity Severity Score (MESS). *J Orthop Trauma* 1994;8(2):81-87.

6. Russell WL, Sailors DM, Whittle TB, Fisher DF Jr, Burns RP: Limb salvage versus traumatic amputation: A decision based on a seven-part predictive index. *Ann Surg* 1991;213(5):473-480, discussion 480-481.

7. Tscherne H, Oestern HJ: A new classification of soft-tissue damage in open and closed fractures (author's transl). *Unfallheilkunde* 1982;85(3):111-115.

8. Bosse MJ, MacKenzie EJ, Kellam JF, et al: A prospective evaluation of the clinical utility of the lower-extremity injury-severity scores. *J Bone Joint Surg Am* 2001;83-A(1):3-14.

9. Ly TV, Travison TG, Castillo RC, Bosse MJ, MacKenzie EJ, LEAP Study Group: Ability of lower-extremity injury severity scores to predict functional outcome after limb salvage. *J Bone Joint Surg Am* 2008;90(8):1738-1743.

10. O'Toole RV, Castillo RC, Pollak AN, MacKenzie EJ, Bosse MJ, LEAP Study Group: Determinants of patient satisfaction after severe lower-extremity injuries. *J Bone Joint Surg Am* 2008;90(6):1206-1211.

11. Gustilo RB, Anderson JT: Prevention of infection in the treatment of one thousand and twenty-five open fractures of long bones: Retrospective and prospective analyses. *J Bone Joint Surg Am* 1976;58(4):453-458.

12. Friedrich PL: Die aseptische Versorgung frischer Wunden. *Arch Klein Chir* 1898;57:288-310.

13. Pollak AN, Castillo RC, Jones AL, Bosse MJ, MacKenzie EJ, LEAP Study Group: Time to definitive treatment significantly influences incidence of infection after open high-energy lower extremity trauma. Annual Scientific Meeting of the Orthopaedic Trauma Association. Salt Lake City, UT, 9 Oct 2003.

14. Skaggs DL, Friend L, Alman B, et al: The effect of surgical delay on acute infection following 554 open fractures in children. *J Bone Joint Surg Am* 2005;87(1):8-12.

15. Spencer J, Smith A, Woods D: The effect of time delay on infection in open long-bone fractures: A 5-year prospective audit from a district general hospital. *Ann R Coll Surg Engl* 2004;86(2):108-112.

16. Bednar DA, Parikh J: Effect of time delay from injury to primary management on the incidence of deep infection after open fractures of the lower extremities caused by blunt trauma in adults. *J Orthop Trauma* 1993;7(6):532-535.

17. Webb LX, Bosse MJ, Castillo RC, MacKenzie EJ, LEAP Study Group: Analysis of surgeon-controlled variables in the treatment of limb-threatening type-III open tibial diaphyseal fractures. *J Bone Joint Surg Am* 2007;89(5):923-928.

18. Yaremchuk MJ, Brumback RJ, Manson PN, Burgess AR, Poka A, Weiland AJ: Acute and definitive management of traumatic osteocutaneous defects of the lower extremity. *Plast Reconstr Surg* 1987;80(1):1-14.

19. Parrett BM, Matros E, Pribaz JJ, Orgill DP: Lower extremity trauma: Trends in the management of soft-tissue reconstruction of open tibia-fibula fractures. *Plast Reconstr Surg* 2006;117(4):1315-1322, discussion 1323-1324.

20. Georgiadis GM, Behrens FF, Joyce MJ, Earle AS, Simmons AL: Open tibial fractures with severe soft-tissue loss: Limb salvage compared with below-the-knee amputation. *J Bone Joint Surg Am* 1993;75(10):1431-1441.

21. Pollak AN, McCarthy ML, Burgess AR; The Lower Extremity Assessment Project (LEAP) Study Group: Short-term wound complications after application of flaps for coverage of traumatic soft-tissue defects about the tibia. *J Bone Joint Surg Am* 2000;82-A(12):1681-1691.

22. Godina M: Early microsurgical reconstruction of complex trauma of the extremities. *Plast Reconstr Surg* 1986;78(3):285-292.

23. Fischer MD, Gustilo RB, Varecka TF: The timing of flap coverage, bone-grafting, and intramedullary nailing in patients who have a fracture of the tibial shaft with extensive soft-tissue injury. *J Bone Joint Surg Am* 1991;73(9):1316-1322.

24. Walters TJ, Kauvar DS, Baer DG, Holcomb JB: Battlefield tourniquets: Modern combat lifesavers. *Army Medical Department Journal* 2005:42-43.

25. Jaicks RR, Cohn SM, Moller BA: Early fracture fixation may be deleterious after head injury. *J Trauma* 1997;42(1):1-5, discussion 5-6.

26. Roberts CS, Pape HC, Jones AL, Malkani AL, Rodriguez JL, Giannoudis PV: Damage control orthopaedics: Evolving concepts in the treatment of patients who have sustained orthopaedic trauma. *Instr Course Lect* 2005;54:447-462.

27. Abramson D, Scalea TM, Hitchcock R, Trooskin SZ, Henry SM, Greenspan J: Lactate clearance and survival following injury. *J Trauma* 1993;35(4):584-588, discussion 588-589.

28. Caudle RJ, Stern PJ: Severe open fractures of the tibia. *J Bone Joint Surg Am* 1987;69(6):801-807.

29. Hansen ST Jr: The type-IIIC tibial fracture: Salvage or amputation. *J Bone Joint Surg Am* 1987;69(6): 799-800.

30. MacKenzie EJ, Bosse MJ, Pollak AN, et al: Long-term persistence of disability following severe lower-limb trauma: Results of a seven-year follow-up. *J Bone Joint Surg Am* 2005;87(8):1801-1809.

Chapter 3

Chronic Neuropathic Pain Following Open Fractures

Marie-Noëlle Hébert-Blouin, MD
Robert J. Spinner, MD

Case Presentation

History

A 25-year-old construction worker was involved in a motorcycle crash with an automobile. On arrival at the emergency department, he had regained consciousness and had a score of 13 on the Glasgow Coma Scale. He had an obvious open soft-tissue deformity of the right leg, which was cool, pale, and without palpable or Doppler-positive pulses at the dorsalis pedis and posterior tibial arteries. The patient had a completely flail right foot with loss of sensation and an open wound in the right distal thigh that showed evidence of a compound fracture. Plain radiographs showed a displaced transverse fracture of the distal femur (**Figure 1**, *A* and *B*). An angiogram showed complete occlusion of the femoral artery at the site of the femoral fracture.

The patient underwent retrograde femoral nailing, fasciotomies, and a vascular repair (**Figure 1**, *C*). He subsequently needed skin grafting over the soft-tissue defects. The patient also had sustained a clavicular fracture, which was treated nonsurgically, and an anterior cruciate ligament (ACL) injury requiring arthroscopy with chondroplasty and ACL reconstruction. Deep vein thrombosis developed later, for which an inferior vena cava filter was inserted. Despite rehabilitation, the patient experienced persistent, severe right sciatic nerve dysfunction and pain.

Current Problem and Management

Eight months after sustaining the open femoral fracture, the patient presented with a posttraumatic right sciatic nerve injury. He reported two types of pain: severe, constant pain that radiated from the region of the distal thigh to the dorsal and plantar aspects of the foot, and mild pain from the surgical incision, extending along the medial aspect of the leg from the thigh to the distal leg to the medial malleolar region. Physical examination showed grade 4 hamstring

Neither of the following authors nor any immediate family member has received anything of value from or owns stock in a commercial company or institution related directly or indirectly to the subject of this article: Dr. Herbert-Blouin and Dr. Spinner.

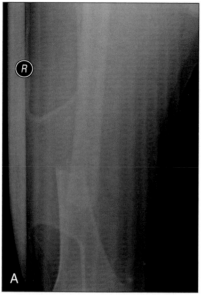

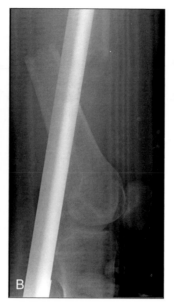

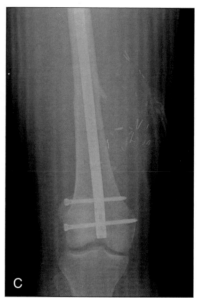

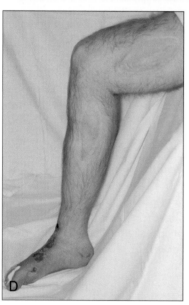

Figure 1 Radiographic images of a 25-year-old man who sustained an open, displaced transverse fracture of the distal femur. AP (**A**) and lateral (**B**) views. **C,** AP radiograph obtained after treatment by closed reduction and internal fixation with an intramedullary nail. **D,** At 2-year follow-up, healed skin grafts from compartment releases are noted and foot ulcers on the insensate foot are apparent. Muscular imbalance from a partially functional tibial division without any peroneal function resulted in a fixed cavovarus foot. The combination of the sensory and motor dysfunction was further complicated by a poorly fitting ankle-foot orthosis, resulting in the problematic ulcerations.

strength, grade 2 gastrocnemius strength, and no posterior tibialis or toe flexion. Peroneal nerve loss was complete, both in superficial and deep distributions. The patient required an ankle-foot orthosis for ambulation. Sensation was absent in the dorsal and plantar aspects of the foot as well as in the saphenous nerve distribution in the leg. No hypersensitivity was present in the foot or leg, and the foot was well vascularized.

On percussion over the sciatic nerve in the distal thigh in the location of the fracture, the patient had moderate pain that radiated toward the popliteal fossa and distally to the foot. In addition, an area over the saphenous nerve near a surgical incision in the medial thigh was sensitive, with radiating paresthesias to the patellar region and the medial leg. Radiographs revealed union of the femoral fracture. Electromyography showed a few units in the medial gastrocnemius and no nascent units in the tibialis anterior, toe extensors, or peronei. Abundant fibrillation potentials were present in the peroneal and tibial innervated muscles.

We diagnosed the source of the patient's neuropathic pain as being twofold: injury to the sciatic nerve (likely from the fracture) and injury to the saphenous nerve (probably from the vascular surgery). The patient was treated nonsurgically with observation, multiple narcotic medications, pregabalin (α^2-∂ ligands, used in this case off-label for neuropathic pain), and muscle relaxants. At 2-year follow-up, the patient had minimal improvement of tibial nerve function, which was insufficient to permit tendon transfer, and no improvement of peroneal nerve function. He continued to use a brace and had developed multiple, infected ulcerations of the foot, which required prolonged antibiotic treatment (**Figure 1, *D***). His neuropathic pain had improved dramatically during the past year. He was weaned from narcotic pain medications and his pain was well controlled at 2-year follow-up with antiepileptic medications, which were gradually being reduced.

DISCUSSION

Chronic pain—neuropathic or musculoskeletal—after open fractures is relatively common and can occur after minor (**Figure 2**) or major (**Figure 3**) bony trauma. Such pain can be debilitating, incapacitating,

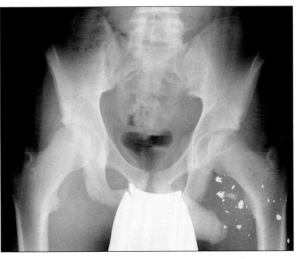

Figure 2   AP pelvic radiograph of a 17-year-old boy who sustained an accidental, self-inflicted gunshot wound to the thigh, resulting in a minor lesser trochanteric fracture. This injury resulted in an incomplete sciatic nerve lesion in the proximal third of the thigh. Pain was well controlled with medications initially; then the medications were discontinued. The patient recovered excellent tibial division function and had incomplete spontaneous recovery of peroneal division function that did not require the use of an ankle-foot orthosis.

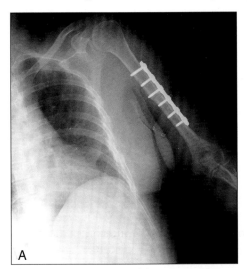

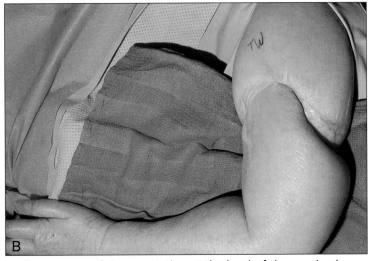

Figure 3   A 59-year-old woman who sustained a near-complete amputation at the level of the proximal third of her left arm in a motor vehicle accident. **A,** AP radiograph obtained after replantation, which was accomplished with bony stabilization and neurovascular reconstruction. **B,** Clinical photograph obtained at 4-month follow-up shows successful replantation. Despite the major trauma, the patient's neuropathic pain was minimal at first and responded well to pharmacologic treatment. She experienced useful neurologic recovery over several years, including distal function.

and difficult to treat. Neuropathic pain must be distinguished from musculoskeletal pain caused by nonunion, malunion, heterotopic ossification, arthritis, or other pathology. This chapter focuses on chronic neuropathic pain after open fractures. The pathophysiology of neuropathic pain is poorly understood, but various inciting injury mechanisms may be involved, including compression, transection, stretch, contusion, crush, and heat injury.

The prevalence of chronic neuropathic pain after open fractures is largely unknown, but it likely occurs more commonly than after closed fractures because of the high-energy forces and the accompanying soft-tissue and bony disruption involved in open fracture. It is not known how a tiny neuroma involving a cutaneous nerve can render a limb dysfunctional whereas a large neuroma involving a major mixed nerve may be asymptomatic. Anecdotal reports exist of an increased prevalence of symptomatic neuromas in certain regions, such as the superficial radial nerve in the distal forearm or the tibial nerve near the ankle, perhaps because of their superficial location in proximity to a joint. Such symptomatic lesions can occur anywhere, however, including deep lesions remote from a joint. Not only are treatment techniques often suboptimal, they also can aggravate or even cause neuropathic pain. Chronic pain has numerous socioeconomic impacts; therefore, attempts to prevent it are at least as important as are those designed to cure it.

Pathophysiology

A neuroma or a neuroma-in-continuity develops when the body regenerates sprouts from the proximal axons in response to complete or partial nerve injury. Neuroma formation is an inevitable response to axotomy and cannot be prevented. The exact mechanisms of neuroma formation are not well understood, however. What is known is that, following a nerve injury of sufficient severity, wallerian degeneration occurs back to the next proximal node of Ranvier, the cell body undergoes chromatolysis, and the reparative process of axonal regeneration ensues. In some cases, the neuroma may comprise functional tissue. In true (stump) neuromas, the process is more disorganized. Lacking endoneurium guidance, regenerating sprouts of proliferative tissue composed of a tangle of axons,

Schwann cells, and fibrocytes in a dense collagenous matrix form bulbous ends of nonfunctional tissue.

It is not well understood why some neuromas become painful and others (fortunately, many) do not. A neuroma may become painful if it is exposed to trauma because of its proximity to skin, a joint, or a scar under tension. Such internal trauma can initiate the mechanical, chemical, or ischemic changes necessary for generating neuropathic pain or dysesthesias. Local neuropeptides released during wallerian degeneration may play a role in the injury response.[1] Membranes of the terminal axonal sprouts can become active spontaneously and act as generators of abnormal electrical activity. One of the mechanisms responsible for this ectopic excitability is the upregulation of sodium channels at the nerve injury site.[1,2]

In neuromas-in-continuity, the pain impulses are initiated by regenerated, unmyelinated nerve fibers. Other mechanisms that may play a role in the genesis of neural pain include impaired blood flow, scarring at the injury bed, nerve compression, or the loss of nerve gliding. Neuropathic pain results from changes in the injured primary sensory neurons and neighboring noninjured sensory neurons, as well as transsynaptic changes in neurons at multiple levels of the central nervous system. The key mechanisms involved include ectopic excitability, phenotypic switch, primary sensory degeneration, central sensitization, and disinhibition.[2]

Recognizing the Problem and High-Risk Situations

The diagnosis of chronic neuropathic pain following an open fracture is often established by history, and it can usually be confirmed by physical examination. In some cases, adjuvant studies or tests may be necessary to establish the diagnosis or eliminate other entities.

In open fractures, the history should ascertain information related to the traumatic event: the mechanism of the injury, the type of fracture, and the type and timing of reduction and fixation. Associated injuries also should be identified. Surgical records should be reviewed and the appearance of the nerve at the time of surgery noted. The timing of the onset of pain should be determined. The pain should be characterized as persistent ("burning"), paroxysmal ("shooting" or "lancinating"), aching, or throbbing, and attempts should be made to quantitate the pain using various outcome measures (eg, a numerical [0-10] rating scale or visual analog scale).

Examination should attempt to pinpoint the area of pain. Elements of stimulus-dependent pain, such as hyperpathia and allodynia, may be present. A complete neurologic examination, including motor, sensory, and autonomic (sweat) testing, should be performed but may not reveal abnormalities. Percussion over nerves in the region of pain should be performed; a positive test will often reveal radiating pain in the distribution of the nerve but, in some cases, only focal tenderness (asymmetric to the contralateral side) may be demonstrated. Active and passive range of motion should be evaluated, and provocative maneuvers that test the nerve or the joint should be done.

Adjunctive studies can help evaluate a pain condition. Electrophysiologic studies, such as electromyography and nerve conduction velocity studies, may determine the location and severity of a lesion. The presence of a nerve injury (even a mild one) in the setting of pain thought to be neuropathic is helpful in pain evaluation. A normal study does not rule out neuropathic pain, however, because electrophysiologic testing does not specifically test pain fibers.

Imaging studies will demonstrate the nature and position of the fracture, which may be helpful in inferring proximity to neighboring nerves. Such studies also will assess fracture union. Nerve abnormalities may be seen on axial CT images or even more clearly on high-resolution MRI. A stump neuroma may appear as an ovoid or heterogeneous focally enlarged mass that is isointense to muscle on T1-weighted images and hyperintense on T2-weighted images, typically nonenhancing with contrast. When needed, subtraction techniques can minimize artifacts from associated hardware. Imaging can reveal not only abnormalities in the nerve, but also other mechanical causes of pain, including structural causes of a neuropathy, such as bony spicule or callus compression, or musculoskeletal issues such as nonunion, malunion, heterotopic ossification, or osteoarthritis. MRI also may help to identify periostitis or soft-tissue edema in chronic regional pain syndrome (CRPS).

Conventional bone scan demonstrates increased uptake at fracture sites in cases of nonunion, and 3-phase bone scan can help to identify infection or CRPS. Noninvasive or invasive vascular studies may be necessary if a pseudoaneurysm is suspected.

Performing and interpreting peripheral nerve blocks, including sympathetic blocks, is often a difficult but important part of the initial examination. Blocks can be done for diagnostic or therapeutic purposes. Rarely, in our experience, do they produce permanent relief. Percutaneous injections of local anesthetic agents (sometimes admixed with steroids) can be done by the surgeon or pain specialist with or without imaging guidance. Administration of the block by another physician removes any potential bias, by either the patient or the physician, which can lead to a misinterpretation of the block. A positive block is helpful but nonspecific. Even more helpful would be a negative block (ie, if an appropriate nerve block has been achieved objectively but resulted in no subjective symptomatic improvement). As part of performing the blocks, which could include placebo blocks (ie, saline or dilute blocks), a patient consent and full disclosure are required.

A differential nerve block is a standard block used to replace placebo blocks; concordant and appropriate temporal responses to either a short- or long-acting agent are expected in true neuropathic pain. Nerve blocks afford the physician the opportunity to establish a patient-physician relationship and to assess the pain response during this intervention. It also allows the patient to experience the numbing effect of the nerve block, in anticipation of a possible neurectomy.

Managing Chronic Pain Following Open Fractures

Several key principles are essential for the effective management of neuropathic pain after open fractures. First, the pain should be diagnosed promptly because the early recognition and treatment of such pain may improve or reverse the pain cycle. Second, a multidisciplinary management approach within the setting of a comprehensive pain clinic is essential. Third, in addition to the physiologic factors, the social and psychological factors affecting the patient also must be identified and addressed. Ideally, the pain mechanism should be considered, and management should target specifically the peripheral or central sites responsible for the pain.

Treatment varies, depending on whether the neuropathic pain is acute or chronic and whether it is caused by a cutaneous nerve, a single major nerve, or multiple major nerves. Treatment may be nonsurgical or surgical. Nonsurgical treatments include psychosocial interventions, rehabilitation, pharmacotherapy, and transcutaneous electrical nerve stimulation (TENS). Useful psychosocial interventions include counseling, relaxation therapy, biofeedback, and support groups. Rehabilitation, when needed, should include physical therapy, massage, acupuncture, desensitization, and contrast baths. The pharmacologic approach includes the use of antidepressants, anticonvulsants, antiarrhythmics, and analgesics administered in various ways. Indications that intensive treatment rather than nonintervention is needed include the patient's escalating use of opiates, the development of depression, and the deterioration of global function. The Short Form Health Survey-36 (SF-36) can be sensitive to such changes, and its use could guide modification of pain treatment.

Surgical options include reconstruction, ablation, and modulation of the peripheral or central nervous system (CNS). The multiple surgical procedures used to treat chronic pain underscore the difficulty of eliminating the problem. Surgical treatment should be tailored to the individual patient because each procedure has its own indications, and no single procedure is suitable for all patients, all types of pain, and all pathologies.

Surgical Treatment: Peripheral Nervous System Approaches

The rationale for treating a neuroma directly is that the neuroma transformed a previous conductor of normal neuronal signals into a generator of abnormal activity. This rationale is strengthened by the fact that injured axons have ectopic discharges, as well as mechanosensitivity and chemosensitivity. Peripheral nervous system treatment approaches attempt to suppress signals at the nerve stump, so the retrograde transport of signals to the cell bodies is disrupted and the regenerative response of cell bodies is inhibited.

Neurolysis

Modification of the environment surrounding a stump neuroma or a neuroma-in-continuity may help relieve chronic pain. For example, relocation of a stump neuroma or neuroma-in-continuity or improving soft-tissue coverage to prevent external (touch) or internal (bone, joint) stimulation may improve the pain of a stump neuroma. In a neuroma-in-continuity, neurolysis and nerve decompression may improve gliding or reduce pressure on the nerve. In select cases, early decompression may benefit patients who are symptomatic because of mass-related compression (eg, from a hematoma or edema). Fibro-osseous tunnels (eg, the carpal or tarsal tunnel), which may be predisposing factors for nerve compression, also may need to be decompressed.

Neuroablation

Simple neurectomy is a common treatment of neuromas involving cutaneous branches. Nerves should be sectioned sharply while under some traction, so that the cut stump will retract (**Figure 4**). Ideally, the nerve stumps should come to rest within an innervated muscle bed with minimal excursion (in a deep plane below the fascia), away from a joint or bone. To prevent or minimize the genesis of a neuroma after simple neurectomy, some experts have advocated supplementary procedures, including ligating or electrocauterizing the stump; performing intraneural injections of alcohol, phenol, or formalin; or inflicting cold or heat injury to the stump. Other authors have proposed capping (**Figure 5**), wrapping, or covering the nerve endings with local or free flaps.[3]

Nerve reconstruction techniques, such as nerve-to-nerve repair, nerve grafts, vein grafts, nerve-tube reconstruction, and even nerve transfers, have been used by some authors to treat pain.[4] Others have tried to minimize neuroma formation by end-to-side or centrocentral anastomosis.[5,6] No method has been able to prevent neuroma formation completely, however.

Neuroaugmenation (Modulation) Therapies

For many patients, peripheral nerve stimulation (PNS) has been a treatment of last resort (**Figure 6**). A recent resurgence of interest in this surgical modality has arisen, however, because of the wider acceptance of neuromodulation as a treatment modality, the introduction of less invasive implantation tech-

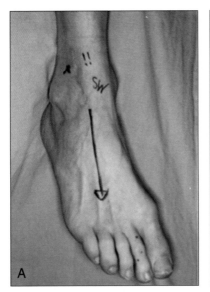 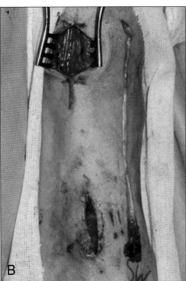

Figure 4   Clinical photographs of the foot of a 42-year-old woman in whom a painful neuroma developed following an open ankle fracture-dislocation. Before treatment, the patient reported painful dysesthesias in the superficial peroneal nerve distribution that became worse with ankle motion. **A,** The foot and ankle are marked for surgery. Percussion at the level of the previous scar caused radiating pain in the direction of the arrow. **B,** After successful nerve blocks were performed for diagnostic purposes, a neurectomy was performed with excellent long-term results. A stump neuroma was identified in the site lateral to the previous incision. A separate proximal incision was made to expose the superficial peroneal nerve. The nerve was sharply transected and buried in a deep site away from the joint. The long segment of resected nerve with its stump neuroma is shown.

niques, and the positive results in the literature. The mechanism of action for this therapy is complex and incompletely understood, but it seems to be related in part to the activation of large A-beta fibers producing a C-fiber inhibition at the level of the substantia gelatinosa.[7] This process validates the gate control theory of Melzack and Wall.[8]

PNS should be considered for neuropathic pain when medical treatments have failed or produce intolerable side effects, when noninterventional therapies have failed, and when further corrective surgery, as described in the previous section, is not expected to be beneficial. Implantable neurostimulation systems are still approved by the US Food and Drug Administration (FDA) only for spinal cord stimulation, so their use for the direct stimulation of peripheral nerves is off-label. To be considered for PNS, in our opinion, a patient should have chronic neuropathic pain that is produced by a single nerve. The most common nerves treated with PNS are the ulnar, median, radial, tibial, and common peroneal nerves. A patient's response to TENS may not predict his or her response to PNS and therefore should not be used to identify patients that are likely to benefit from this modality. A suitable PNS patient is one who has adequate motivation and a clear understanding that PNS may help to control chronic neuropathic pain but will not cure the underlying disease process. The patient should not have any medical contraindications or significant alcohol or drug dependence.[7,9] A successful stimulation trial (>50% improvement in pain intensity) helps identify patients who will benefit from a neurostimulation system.

PNS requires familiarity with special techniques and equipment. Implantation is more labor intensive than the use of a spinal cord stimulator, but new percutaneous techniques are being developed. The rate for significant complications is low, but a relatively high rate of mechanical failure exists, with lead migration occurring in up to 20% of patients with the percutaneous technique.[7,9] The

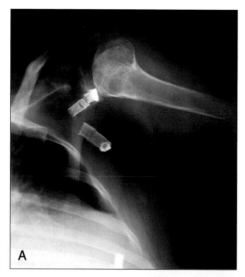

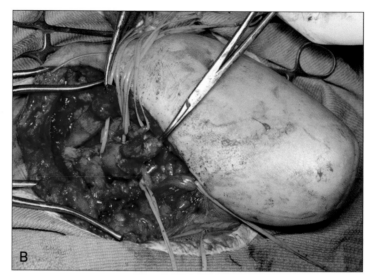

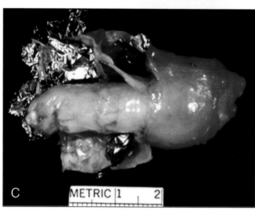

Figure 5 Painful stump neuromas and phantom pain in a 52-year-old man after amputation of the left arm immediately following severe trauma. Attempts at controlling his neuropathic pain included neurectomies and subsequent capping of the neuroma stumps with Teflon caps. **A,** AP radiograph showing capping of the stumps. **B,** Intraoperative photograph taken during a later operation in which the stumps were resected more proximally. At 3-year follow-up, the patient reported 75% improvement. **C,** Clinical photograph showing part of the resected stump. The Teflon caps placed to prevent neuroma formation resulted in constriction of the nerve (left side of the figure) but bulbous neuroma formation still occurred more proximally (right side of the figure).

goals of PNS are to improve pain, sleep, and functional activity, and to reduce the use of medication. Recent series report good or excellent outcomes in 60% to 65% of patients, including pain reduction and improvement in functional activity and in quality of life. Some patients have even returned to work.[10,11] The success of this technique lies in careful patient selection.

Surgical Treatment: Central Nervous System Approaches

When chronic neuropathic pain is refractory to all treatment modalities, neuromodulation or neuroablation of CNS components can be used to treat the pain. In general, the advantage of neuromodulation

procedures over neuroablative procedures is their reversibility and safety. In the CNS, the two targets for the treatment of chronic neuropathic pain are the spinal cord and the brain.

Neuromodulation of the Spinal Cord
Spinal cord stimulation (SCS) has been used for several years to treat a variety of chronic pain conditions, including CRPS types I and II and peripheral nerve injury (including that resulting from brachial plexus injury and stump/phantom pain). SCS may be appropriate when neuropathic pain is caused by multiple nerve injuries (**Figure 7**). SCS is FDA-approved in the management of chronic, intractable pain of the trunk or limbs associated with various conditions, including CRPS. The stimulation is achieved via epidural electrodes at C4 or C5 for upper extremity

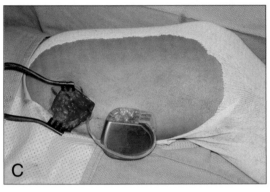

Figure 6   A 50-year-old woman sustained an open ankle fracture-dislocation; severe tibial nerve pain developed subsequently. Multiple operations performed elsewhere on the neuroma failed to improve her symptoms. She was felt to be a good candidate for peripheral nerve stimulation. **A,** During the operation, the neuroma is identified. **B,** The electrode is placed under the tibial nerve proximal to the neuroma. **C,** The pulse generator is positioned in the distal thigh. Five-year follow-up has documented significant improvements in her overall pain and function. She has not taken pain medication since the stimulator placement.

pain and at T9 to T11 for lower extremity pain. The stimulation produces paresthesias over the body part that correspond to the spinal cord segment being stimulated. The mechanism of action of SCS, like PNS, is based on the gate control theory of pain transmission, but it has not yet been fully elucidated.[8,12] The complication rate associated with SCS insertion is 20% to 30%, but major complications are rare and most complications are device related (lead migration, fracture, etc.).[13,14] Case study reports of the results of SCS for the treatment of pain in CRPS type I and II and peripheral nerve injuries are promising: 67% to 85% of patients reported significant improvement in functional capacity and quality of life.[12-14] Confirmatory comparative trials are needed, however.

Neuromodulation also can be achieved through the delivery of spinal intrathecal medications. Of all spinally administered analgesics, preservative-free morphine sulfate remains the current gold standard and is the only opioid approved by the FDA for intrathecal delivery to treat chronic pain.[15] Preservative-free ziconotide, a neuronal-specific, N-gated calcium channel blocker working at the dorsal horn, also is FDA approved for chronic intrathecal infusion used in the management of severe chronic pain. Alternative drugs have been used off-label for intrathecal therapy, however, either alone or in combination, including hydromorphone, baclofen (FDA-approved for spasticity but used off-label for pain), local anesthetics such as bupivacaine, and α² agonists such as clonidine. Intrathecal medication delivery is a therapeutic option for patients in whom all other treatments have failed, and for those in whom adequate analgesia is achieved by a high oral dose of medications but with unacceptable side effects.[15] Intrathecal opioids act directly on receptors in the substantia gelatinosa of the spinal cord dorsal horn, providing a dose-dependent analgesia.[16] At up to 4-year follow-up, 50% to 75% of patients with mixed nociceptive deafferentation or neuropathic non-cancer pain achieve fair or good pain relief.[17,18] Further studies are needed, however, to identify which pain conditions or subpopulations of patients are most responsive to treatment with intrathecal opioids and which agent or combination of agents is

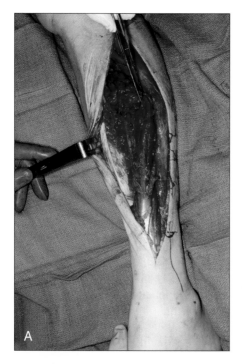

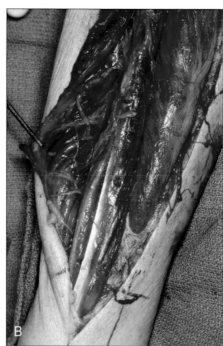

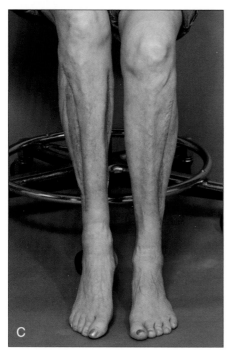

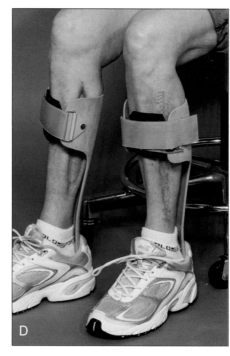

Figure 7 Clinical photographs of a 65-year-old woman with bilateral lower limb compartment syndromes that necessitated compartment releases (**A**), and muscular débridements (**B**). The patient had bilateral foot drops (**C**), which were controlled by bracing (**D**). She also developed severe bilateral neuropathic pain. She was felt to be a good candidate for spinal cord stimulation, but she was not interested in pursuing this option in view of her multiple previous surgeries and failed attempts at other pain interventions.

most appropriate for each situation.[15] Complications of intrathecal infusion therapy include infection, pump or catheter failure, medication side effects, and granuloma formation.

Neuroablation of the Spinal Cord

The main neuroablative procedure used in patients with peripheral nerve lesions is dorsal root entry zone (DREZ) lesioning. The basis of DREZ lesioning is to stop the excessive firing of the dorsal horn neurons that leads to pain.[19] It mainly is used for patients having chronic deafferentation pain, such as in brachial plexus avulsion injuries. When patients are selected carefully and the lesioning is performed accurately, the initial success rate can be as high as 66% to 90% at up to 4-year follow-up,[19,20] with longer follow-up showing a decrease in efficacy to 50%.[21]

Neuromodulation of the Brain

Motor cortex stimulation, using implantable neurostimulation systems off-label, may be used for neuropathic limb pain. The reported success rate is around 50% in case reports and small case series.[12,22] Deep-brain stimulation of the sensory thalamus and periventricular gray matter, using the same devices off-label, also has been successful in some patients,[12] although it is more effective for nociceptive pain than for neuropathic pain (63% versus 47% long-term success).[23] In patients with neuropathic pain, however, moderately higher rates of success are seen in those with peripheral lesions (phantom limb pain, radiculopathies, plexopathies, and neuropathies) than in those with CNS lesions.[23]

Preventing Chronic Pain Following Open Fractures

Chronic pain is defined as the lasting perception of pain long after tissue healing has occurred and in the absence of a documented cause for pain.[24] The reason chronic pain develops in some patients and not in others after an injury such as an open fracture is not well understood. The main processes hypothesized to be involved in the transition from an acute to a chronic pain state are nerve hyperexcitability and central sensitization.[24] Although psychosocial variables appear to be the most potent predictors of many chronic pain

syndromes, biomedical variables also may be important predictors in the multiple-trauma population.[24,25] Such biomedical predictors for the development of chronic pain include the site and extent of surgery; the need for multiple operations; and the occurrence of postsurgical infection, bleeding, compartment syndrome, or unrelieved pain.[25]

The timely management and thoughtful care of patients with open fractures can reduce the incidence of chronic pain. Moreover, the avoidance of injury following trauma—especially during and after surgery—is crucial. Intraoperative factors that can minimize the incidence of chronic pain include a good knowledge of anatomy and of the common anatomic variations, careful surgical planning, and good technique. Postoperatively, the avoidance of nerve compression secondary to edema, hematoma, infection, or a tight dressing is also essential.

The insight that pain is more than a consequence of wounding and may be a disease process in itself has led to an emphasis on effective acute pain management.[25,26] Effective pain control could positively affect recovery following trauma and reduce long-term morbidity.[26] This understanding has led to the development of preventive analgesia to reduce the central sensitization that arises from noxious inputs experienced throughout the entire perioperative period. Preemptive treatment directed at the peripheral sensory axons and the central neurons can be accomplished with nonsteroidal anti-inflammatory drugs, acetaminophen, local anesthetics, α^2-agonists (eg, clonidine), α^2-∂ ligands (eg, gabapentin and pregabalin), ketamine, or opioids.[27] The use of these drugs for preventive analgesia is mainly off-label. Several authors have reported using perioperative preventive epidural analgesia over several days to reduce the incidence of phantom pain after amputation, but contradictory results and multiple flaws in study design have prevented the drawing of any conclusions about the efficacy of this technique in preventing the development of phantom pain.[27] We occasionally use a similar approach—several days of intravenous analgesia surrounding cutaneous neuroma resection or neurolysis—in patients undergoing corrective surgeries for painful neuromas.

A recent development in the treatment of acute pain, developed in response to the growing number of seriously injured soldiers returning from US military operations in Iraq, is the aggressive early use of advanced regional anesthesia. Techniques developed for regional anesthesia on the battlefield and during the evacuation of patients with injured limbs include peripheral nerve blocks, continuous infusion peripheral nerve catheters, and patient-controlled anesthesia. These techniques use peripheral nerve stimulation or ultrasound to facilitate the accurate placement of needles in the proximity of targeted nerves, including the brachial plexus, so that local anesthetic can be injected to block the conduction of these nerves.[24] Alternatively, a continuous peripheral nerve block can be established for a period of days to weeks.[24] These regional anesthesia techniques provide excellent postoperative analgesia, reducing narcotic use and potentially reducing the incidence of chronic pain syndromes.[28] Such techniques are presently used for combat injuries, but they could potentially be applied to civilian traumatic injuries such as open fractures.

The impact of these techniques on the incidence and severity of posttraumatic neuropathic pain remains unclear, however. Animal models suggest that traumatic nerve injury left untreated causes "central sensitization" or neural remodeling that can ultimately lead to a state of sustained or chronic neuropathic pain,[1] but little is known about the importance of prompt and effective pain relief in humans. Further studies are needed to explore these and other techniques and their role in preventing the development of chronic pain.

The successful treatment of patients with neuropathic pain remains one of the most rewarding aspects of our peripheral nerve practices. Patients with neuropathic pain benefit from a multidisciplinary but individualized approach. Those nonresponsive or minimally responsive to nonsurgical measures may benefit from consideration of surgical interventions. In general, for any given procedure, 60% to 70% of treated patients will experience improvement in pain control. The long-term results may not be as good, however. Success depends on accurate patient selection, which is not as easy as it seems. In general, we give patients a 50/50 chance of long-term success following surgical intervention. Poor indicators for success include multiple previous operations and ongoing workers' compensation negotiations or litigation.

CASE MANAGEMENT AND OUTCOME

Eight months after the open femur fracture, the patient presented with posttraumatic sciatic nerve injury. He showed minimal reinnervation signs (only in the tibial division) and had neuropathic pain. Two issues equally concerned the patient: function and pain.

This type of injury historically has produced poor functional results. Considering the mechanism (a longitudinal stretch injury), location (the thigh), and timing of the combined neurovascular injury, the outcomes for reconstruction of the peroneal division were felt to be poor. Results following nerve grafting to the peroneal nerve division of the sciatic nerve are disappointing even under the best of circumstances. The paucity of donors would make opportunities for distal nerve transfer implausible. Free functioning muscle transfer in this setting has had poor outcomes. The only viable option for functional improvement was a tendon transfer for foot dorsiflexion if the posterior tibialis tendon recovered further strength. Unfortunately, but not surprisingly, it did not.

The neuropathic pain slowly resolved without surgical treatment, however. If the pain had persisted, we would have tried to determine the nerves responsible. Neurolysis of the sciatic nerve could have been considered either alone or in combination with a resection of the saphenous nerve neuroma. If the pain had been refractory to these surgical approaches, it might have responded to spinal cord stimulation.

REFERENCES

1. Baron R: Mechanisms of disease: Neuropathic pain—A clinical perspective. *Nat Clin Pract Neurol* 2006;2:95-106.
2. Woolf CJ: Dissecting out mechanisms responsible for peripheral neuropathic pain: Implications for diagnosis and therapy. *Life Sci* 2004;74:2605-2610.
3. Yüksel F, Kişlaoğlu E, Durak N, Uçar C, Karacaoğlu E: Prevention of painful neuromas by epineurial ligatures, flaps and grafts. *Br J Plast Surg* 1997;50:182-185.
4. Berman J, Anand P, Chen L, Taggart M, Birch R: Pain relief from preganglionic injury to the brachial plexus

by late intercostal nerve transfer. *J Bone Joint Surg Br* 1996;78:759-760.

5. Al-Qattan MM: Prevention and treatment of painful neuromas of the superficial radial nerve by the end-to-side nerve repair concept: An experimental study and preliminary clinical experience. *Microsurgery* 2000; 20:99-104.

6. Barberá J, Albert-Pampló R: Centrocentral anastomosis of the proximal nerve stump in the treatment of painful amputation neuromas of major nerves. *J Neurosurg* 1993;79:331-334.

7. Weiner RL: Peripheral nerve neurostimulation. *Neurosurg Clin N Am* 2003;14:401-408.

8. Melzack R, Wall PD: Pain mechanisms: A new theory. *Science* 1965;150:971-979.

9. Slavin KV: Peripheral nerve stimulation for neuropathic pain. *Neurotherapeutics* 2008;5:100-106.

10. Mobbs RJ, Nair S, Blum P: Peripheral nerve stimulation for the treatment of chronic pain. *J Clin Neurosci* 2007;14:216-221.

11. Novak CB, Mackinnon SE: Outcome following implantation of a peripheral nerve stimulator in patients with chronic nerve pain. *Plast Reconstr Surg* 2000;105:1967-1972.

12. Cruccu G, Aziz TZ, Garcia-Larrea L: EFNS guidelines on neurostimulation therapy for neuropathic pain. *Eur J Neurol* 2007;14:952-970.

13. Cameron T: Safety and efficacy of spinal cord stimulation for the treatment of chronic pain: A 20-year literature review. *J Neurosurg* 2004;100(3 suppl spine):254-267.

14. Taylor RS, Van Buyten JP, Buchser E: Spinal cord stimulation for complex regional pain syndrome: A systematic review of the clinical and cost-effectiveness literature and assessment of prognostic factors. *Eur J Pain* 2006; 10:91-101.

15. Smith HS, Deer TR, Staats PS, Singh V, Sehgal N, Cordner H: Intrathecal drug delivery. *Pain Physician* 2008;11:S89-S104.

16. Pert CB, Snyder SH: Opiate receptor: Demonstration in nervous tissue. *Science* 1973;179:1011-1014.

17. Anderson VC, Burchiel KJ: A prospective study of long-term intrathecal morphine in the management of chronic nonmalignant pain. *Neurosurgery* 1999;44:289-300.

18. Kumar K, Kelly M, Pirlot T: Continuous intrathecal morphine treatment for chronic pain of nonmalignant etiology: Long-term benefits and efficacy. *Surg Neurol* 2001;55:79-86.

19. Raslan AM, McCartney S, Burchiel KJ: Management of chronic severe pain: Spinal neuromodulatory and neuroablative approaches. *Acta Neurochir Suppl* 2007; 97:33-41.

20. Sindou MP, Blondet E, Emery E, Mertens P: Microsurgical lesioning in the dorsal root entry zone for pain due to brachial plexus avulsion: A prospective series of 55 patients. *J Neurosurg* 2005;102:1018-1028.

21. Chen HJ, Tu YK: Long term follow-up results of dorsal root entry zone lesions for intractable pain after brachial plexus avulsion injuries. *Acta Neurochir Suppl* 2006;99:73-75.

22. Nuti C, Peyron R, Garcia-Larrea L: Motor cortex stimulation for refractory neuropathic pain: Four year outcome and predictors of efficacy. *Pain* 2005;118:43-52.

23. Bittar RG, Kar-Purkayastha I, Owen SL: Deep brain stimulation for pain relief: A meta-analysis. *J Clin Neurosci* 2005;12:515-519.

24. Clark ME, Bair MJ, Buckenmaier CC, Gironda RJ, Walker RL: Pain and combat injuries in soldiers returning from Operations Enduring Freedom and Iraqi Freedom: Implications for research and practice. *J Rehabil Res Dev* 2007;44:179-194.

25. Shipton EA, Tait B: Flagging the pain: Preventing the burden of chronic pain by identifying and treating risk factors in acute pain. *Eur J Anaesthesiol* 2005; 22:405-412.

26. Carr DB, Goudas LC: Acute pain. *Lancet* 1999;353: 2051-2058.

27. Reuben SS, Buvanendran A: Preventing the development of chronic pain after orthopaedic surgery with preventive multimodal analgesic techniques. *J Bone Joint Surg Am* 2007;89:1343-1358.

28. Baker BC, Buckenmaier CT, Narine N, Compeggie ME, Brand GJ, Mongan PD: Battlefield anesthesia: Advances in patient care and pain management. *Anesthesiol Clin* 2007;25:131-145.

Chapter 4

Management of Soft-Tissue Loss After Trauma

Milan K. Sen, MD, FRCSC
Edward J. Harvey, MD, MSc

Introduction

High-energy trauma to the extremities results in a challenging variety of orthopaedic injuries, usually associated with varying degrees of soft-tissue injury.[1-6] A soft-tissue defect may result from the initial event or from débridement. The outcome of managing bony injuries or salvaging the limb is often determined by the soft-tissue loss.[7-9] In such situations, the orthopaedic surgeon must be not only a good fracture surgeon but also an adept and knowledgeable manager of soft-tissue defects. This chapter presents several case histories that illustrate some of the currently available soft-tissue treatment options, such as negative pressure wound therapy, dermal substitutes, pedicle flaps, and free flaps.

The Reconstructive Ladder

In 1980, Mathes[10] used the term *reconstructive ladder* to describe a series of steps in the reconstructive process, beginning with the simplest procedures at the bottom of the ladder and progressing to the more complex ones toward the top. New developments that permit successful limb salvage using less complex and invasive techniques, such as negative pressure wound therapy and dermal substitutes, have added more rungs at the bottom of the ladder. The cases presented in this chapter illustrate various available treatment options. An evolution in thought has occurred regarding several treatment procedures, including the primary closure of wounds and revised pedicle flaps. This evolution in thought states that primary closure and the use of hardware in an open fracture are safe. New techniques, such

Milan K. Sen, MD, FRCSC, or a member of his immediate family has received research or institutional support and miscellaneous nonincome support (such as equipment or services), commercially derived honoraria, or other non-research-related funding (such as paid travel) from Synthes and Stryker. Edward J. Harvey, MD, MSc, or a member of his immediate family has received research or institutional support from Synthes Canada, Zimmer, and Stryker.

as dermal substitutes (illustrated in case 1) and vacuum-assisted closure, also have been added to the surgeon's suite of treatment options.

Initial Management of Soft-Tissue Injuries

Traumatic wounds, especially those that are contaminated or associated with open fractures, should be débrided on an urgent basis. Soft-tissue–friendly fracture techniques should be used for stabilization; their type and timing are determined by the condition of the soft tissues and the extent of contamination. Aggressive débridement of traumatic wounds, along with the realization that all devitalized tissue—skin as well as subcutaneous fat, fascia, muscle, tendon, and bone—must be excised, is paramount for safe treatment.[6,11] The surgeon must treat the devitalized area like a locally aggressive tumor, preserving neurovascular tissues and joint surfaces but excising the affected tissue. Bone that is devoid of any soft-tissue attachments will only serve as a sequestrum for bacteria and will not help the eventual reconstruction. The current thought is that primary wound closure is the safest option for most wounds without skin loss, so surgeons must look before they leap.[12-14] Using a treatment algorithm (**Figure 1**) modeled after a reconstructive ladder, we have reduced the number of free-tissue and flap transfer procedures in our institutions by considering the simplest procedures first. [15,16]

Only after the initial débridement can the surgeon accurately assess the extent of the soft-tissue injury and the patient's reconstructive needs. Consideration should be given to the size and location of the defect, the type of tissue that is exposed, the condition of the local tissues, and any patient comorbidities.

The Orthoplastic Team Approach

Management of soft-tissue loss associated with open fractures requires cooperation between the orthopaedic surgeon, who is often the primary surgeon, and the reconstructive microsurgeon or plastic surgeon. Levin and Condit[11] have called this cooperative arrangement the "orthoplastic" approach. Early involvement of the microsurgeon is vital so that a comprehensive and coordinated plan can be devel-

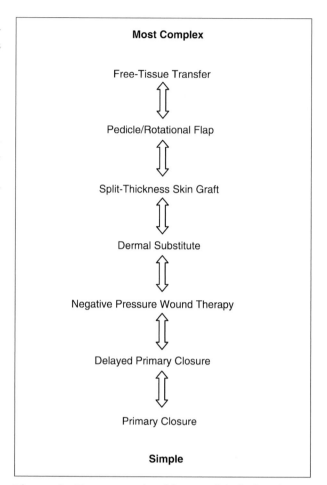

Figure 1 Treatment algorithm modeled after the modern reconstructive ladder.

oped for management of both the bony and soft-tissue injuries. Such a plan facilitates early coverage, shortens the overall reconstructive time, and minimizes mistakes that can jeopardize limb salvage.[1,2,8,10,17-19] Cooperation is particularly important when planning incisions, débridements, and placement of internal or external hardware (**Figure 2**). Circumstances in which a microsurgeon is unavailable will certainly arise, however. Early consultation is important in such cases, even if it requires bundling patients and their wounds in biologic dressings and transferring them to a more appropriate treatment center. The use of vacuum-assisted closure does not replace adequate assessment, even though it may adequately replace a microsurgical procedure in the long run.

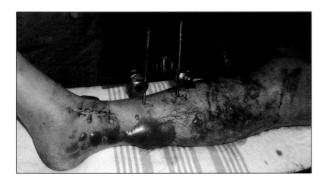

Figure 2   Clinical photograph of the right leg of a patient who sustained a tibial plateau fracture and degloving of the leg. Initial plans had been to perform open reduction and internal fixation, but the procedure would have resulted in sloughing of the skin of the entire leg. Fine pin fixation was chosen as an alternative. Additional treatment included repeat débridements, a pedicled soleus flap, and a skin graft. Early planning and good communication between the microsurgeon and the orthopaedic surgeon saved this patient from amputation.

CASE 1: NEGATIVE PRESSURE WOUND THERAPY AND DERMAL SUBSTITUTES

History

A 43-year-old man was involved in a motorcycle accident in which he sustained an open dislocation of the Lisfranc joint with fractures of the 2nd, 3rd, 4th, and 5th metatarsals. His orthopaedic injuries were isolated to the foot.

Management

Initial management included open reduction and internal fixation (ORIF) of the Lisfranc injury and percutaneous stabilization of the metatarsal fractures. After multiple débridements, a 12-cm × 15-cm wound remained on the dorsum of the foot with exposed tendons and some exposed bone (**Figure 3, A**). A dermal substitute was applied with negative pressure wound therapy (**Figure 3, B**). Ten days later, the wound was covered with a split-thickness skin graft. The graft was

100% viable and produced a good cosmetic result (**Figure 3, C**).

Discussion

Negative (or subatmospheric) pressure wound therapy applies subatmospheric pressure to a wound in a closed system to promote granulation and wound healing.[20] It is believed to accomplish this task by removing exudates and slough, reducing the bacterial load, providing a moist wound environment, reducing edema, and increasing blood flow (and therefore growth factors, white blood cells, and fibroblasts) to the wound. Negative pressure wound therapy has become commonplace because of its supposed cost effectiveness and a perceived lack of need for specialty care.

A wide variety of dermal substitutes are available commercially. Some are derived from human tissue and others from animal tissue. They typically consist of collagen and other extracellular matrix proteins and provide a scaffold for tissue ingrowth.[21,22] In the management of orthopaedic wounds, dermal substitutes can provide a layer of tissue that adds bulk underneath split-thickness skin grafts and minimizes adhesions between the skin graft and underlying tendons or neurovascular structures. As illustrated in case 1, the bulk provided by this tissue also results in improved appearance of the graft in some situations

CASE 2: PEDICLE FLAPS

History

An 85-year-old man who tried to push his stalled car was struck on the knee by the car and then dragged along the asphalt. He sustained an open patellar fracture with a 6-cm × 6-cm wound. Asphalt was embedded in the patella.

Management

The patient was taken to the operating room on an urgent basis for irrigation and débridement, ORIF with transosseous sutures, and primary wound closure. On postoperative day 7, he underwent repeat irrigation and débridement for a wound infection. Frank pus was tracking from the wound into the knee joint. Multiple irrigation and débridements, with partial débridement

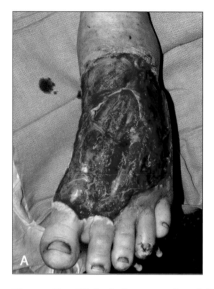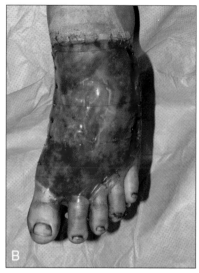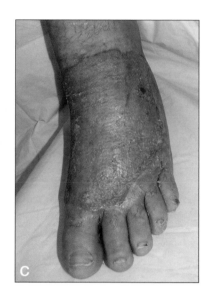

Figure 3 Clinical photographs of the foot of the patient described in case 1, who sustained an open Lisfranc dislocation and fractures of metatarsals 2 through 5. **A,** After multiple débridements, a 12-cm × 15-cm wound remained on the dorsum of the foot with exposed tendons and some bone. This injury would usually necessitate free-tissue transfer or split-thickness skin graft with attendant tendon tethering. **B,** A dermal substitute was applied with negative pressure wound therapy. **C,** Ten days later, the wound was covered with a split-thickness skin graft, which produced a good cosmetic result.

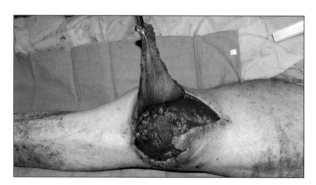

Figure 4 Open patellar fracture of the right leg in the 85-year-old man described in case 2.

of the patellar tendon and bone, were necessary to remove the infected tissue, and the patient was left with an 8-cm × 8-cm wound on the anterior aspect of his knee. The quadriceps tendon, patellar tendon, and patellar bone were exposed, but the extensor mechanism was intact (**Figure 4**). The wound was managed with a pedicled medial gastrocnemius rotation flap and a split-thickness skin graft. This flap is typically used for cov-erage of defects involving the proximal tibia, but release of its origin off the posterior femur and passage underneath the hamstring tendons allow for enough excursion to cover the knee. The wound healed without incident.

Discussion

Pedicle flaps are a suitable option in some lower extremity trauma cases. The rule of thirds—which recommends gastrocnemius flaps for defects involving the proximal third of the tibia, soleus flaps for those involving the middle third, and free flaps for those involving the distal third—still generally holds true. An advantage of pedicle flaps is their familiarity to many orthopaedic surgeons. They also do not require microsurgical technique. New types of pedicle flap techniques have begun to be used by orthopaedic surgeons, including the mobilization of classic simple pedicle flaps, such as was done in case 2, to increase the reach and diversify the indications for these flaps. Innovative flaps and new uses for pedicle flaps also have increased the armamentarium of the microsurgeon.[11,17] For example, the reverse sural artery flap, posterior tibial artery perforator flap, dorsalis pedis flap, and others now can cover the distal third of the tibia—an area where only free flaps traditionally have been used. The decision whether to use these types of flaps for defects around the ankle depends on the size of the area that needs to be covered. An additional concern is that the local tissue in this area lies within the zone of injury and is traumatized. The blood supply to these types of flap is not as robust as is the blood supply to the true muscle flaps, and problems with flap necrosis and venous congestion can occur. Care must be taken in the use of such flaps, but they certainly can be useful in averting morbidity and amputation in some lower extremity wounds.

CASE 3: FREE FLAP FOR DEGLOVING INJURY
History

A 33-year-old man was traveling at high speed when his motorcycle skidded out from under him. His left foot and ankle were caught between the motorcycle and the guardrail and he sustained a degloving injury to the anterolateral aspect of his foot, a bimalleolar ankle fracture-dislocation, and a calcaneocuboid dislocation. The wound measured 15 cm × 20 cm and involved the skin, subcutaneous tissues, extensor digitorum brevis muscle, and extensor digitorum longus tendons 2 through 5 (**Figure 5**, *A*).

Management

Several débridements were performed. The wound was covered on postinjury day 4 with a rectus abdominus free flap and split-thickness skin graft (**Figure 5**, *B*). This type of free flap was chosen because of the peripheral wound, which had little local tissue to ensure large wound coverage. The wound healed without incident.

Discussion

Free flaps have several advantages over pedicle flaps. Abundant donor tissue is available for free flaps, making them more versatile for coverage of large defects. Additionally, the tissue is taken from outside the zone of injury. The disadvantages of using free flaps are the

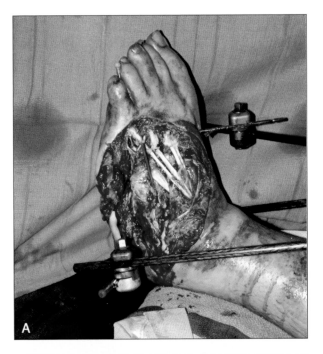

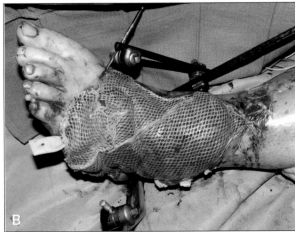

Figure 5 Clinical photographs of the foot of the 33-year-old man described in case 3, who sustained a bimalleolar ankle fracture-dislocation, a calcaneocuboid dislocation, and a degloving injury to the anterolateral aspect of the left foot. **A,** The wound measured 15 cm × 20 cm and involved the skin, subcutaneous tissues, extensor digitorum brevis muscle, and extensor digitorum longus tendons 2 through 5. **B,** After several débridements, the wound was covered on postinjury day 4 with a rectus abdominus free flap and a split-thickness skin graft.

additional donor site morbidity and the need for micro-surgical techniques requiring considerably longer and more complicated surgery. Two types of free flaps are commonly used for coverage of orthopaedic injuries: muscle flaps and fasciocutaneous flaps. Although fascio-cutaneous flaps, such as the anterolateral thigh flap, are gaining in popularity, the muscle flap remains the gold standard because it is believed to provide increased vascularity, resulting in better oxygen and antibiotic delivery.[6,23,24] The muscle flap also is better at contouring and filling dead space.

The rectus abdominus muscle is a commonly used free muscle flap. It is easily harvested, has large-caliber vessels for anastomosis, and can cover a large area. The length of its intramuscular pedicle allows for anastomosis to recipient vessels that are more remote from the site of injury. Other muscles often used for free-tissue transfer in orthopaedic trauma are the latissimus dorsi and gracilis muscles.

CASE 4: FREE FLAP FOR TRAUMATIC AMPUTATION
History

A 31-year-old man was involved in a motorcycle accident that resulted in a traumatic amputation through the tibia and fibula of the left leg at the mid-diaphyseal level.

Management

The femur fracture initially was managed with a reamed, locked intramedullary nail, and the traumatic amputation was treated with a guillotine amputation of the tibia (**Figure 6, A**). After several débridements and negative pressure wound therapy, healthy muscle tissue was found to be present, but it was not sufficient to cover the minimal tibial length necessary to salvage a below-knee amputation. It was believed that a below-knee amputation would be better than a knee disartic-ulation or above-knee amputation, so a free rectus abdominus muscle flap was used to cover the stump and preserve tibial length. The patient recovered very well and now has a well-functioning residual limb (**Figure 6, B**).

Discussion

The preservation of length in a traumatic amputation is controversial. The dangers of infection, the risks of surgery in the zone of injury, and the inherent vessel compromise lead many surgeons to choose straight amputation. After early demarcation of the wound accompanied by aggressive local wound management,

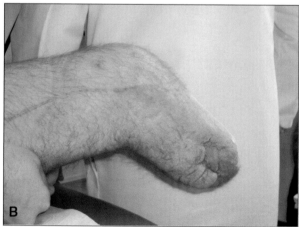

Figure 6 Clinical photographs of the leg of the 31-year-old man described in case 4 who sustained a traumatic below-knee amputation of the left leg. **A,** After several débridements and negative pressure wound therapy, healthy muscle tissue was present, but it was not sufficient to cover the minimal tibial length necessary to salvage a below-knee amputation. **B,** The residual limb after treatment. A free rectus abdominus muscle flap was used to cover the stump and preserve tibial length.

preservation or elongation of the terminal viable leg is possible, however. Certainly the outcomes of any amputation are poor but the relative easier management and decreased oxygen requirements of a below-knee amputation make this treatment a better option for the patient.

Strategies for Managing Soft-Tissue Loss

Successful management of soft-tissue loss is critical in the treatment of high-energy extremity trauma. Cooperation with a reconstructive microsurgeon is an important step in early injury management and can help to avoid common complications of such injuries. The reconstructive ladder can help guide the orthopaedic surgeon and direct treatment, and the development of new technologies has helped simplify the management of certain wounds. When possible, the least invasive technique that can provide an acceptable outcome should be used. More complex procedures are warranted when the simpler techniques fail or when the size or location of the defect necessitates them, with free-tissue transfer as the definitive solution.

References

1. Byrd HS, Cierny GI III, Tebbetts JB: The management of open tibial fractures with associated soft-tissue loss: External pin fixation with early flap coverage. *Plast Reconstr Surg* 1981;68(1):73-82.

2. Cierny G III, Byrd HS, Jones RE: Primary versus delayed soft tissue coverage for severe open tibial fractures: A comparison of results. *Clin Orthop Relat Res* 1983;178:54-63.

3. DeLong WG Jr, Born CT, Wei SY, Petrik ME, Ponzio R, Schwab CW: Aggressive treatment of 119 open fracture wounds. *J Trauma* 1999;46(6):1049-1054.

4. Gustilo RB, Anderson JT: Prevention of infection in the treatment of one thousand and twenty-five open fractures of long bones: Retrospective and prospective analyses. *J Bone Joint Surg Am* 1976;58(4):453-458.

5. Hohmann E, Tetsworth K, Radziejowski MJ, Wiesniewski TF: Comparison of delayed and primary wound closure in the treatment of open tibial fractures. *Arch Orthop Trauma Surg* 2007;127(2):131-136.

6. Hampton OP Jr: Management of open fractures and open wounds of joints. 1968. *Clin Orthop Relat Res* 1997;345:4-7.

7. Gustilo RB, Merkow RL, Templeman D: The management of open fractures. *J Bone Joint Surg Am* 1990;72(2):299-304.

8. Olson S: Open fractures of the tibial shaft: Current treatment. *Instr Course Lect* 1996;78:1428-1437.

9. Sanders R, Swiontkowski M, Nunley J, Spiegel P: The management of fractures with soft-tissue disruptions. *J Bone Joint Surg Am* 1993;75(5):778-789.

10. Mathes SJ, Alpert BS: Advances in muscle and musculocutaneous flaps. *Clin Plast Surg* 1980;7(1):15-26.

11. Levin LS, Condit DP: Combined injuries—soft tissue management. *Clin Orthop Relat Res* 1996;327:172-181.

12. Benson DR, Riggins RS, Lawrence RM, Hoeprich PD, Huston AC, Harrison JA: Treatment of open fractures: A prospective study. *J Trauma* 1983;23(1):25-30.

13. Russell GG, Henderson R, Arnett G: Primary or delayed closure for open tibial fractures. *J Bone Joint Surg Br* 1990;72(1):125-128.

14. Weitz-Marshall AD, Bosse MJ: Timing of closure of open fractures. *J Am Acad Orthop Surg* 2002;10(6):379-384.

15. Levin LS: The reconstructive ladder: An orthoplastic approach. *Orthop Clin North Am* 1993;24(3):393-409.

16. Godina M: Early microsurgical reconstruction of complex trauma of the extremities. *Plast Reconstr Surg* 1986;78(3):285-292.

17. Heller L, Levin LS: Lower extremity microsurgical reconstruction. *Plast Reconstr Surg* 2001;108(4):1029-1041, quiz 1042.

18. Hertel R, Lambert SM, Müller S, Ballmer FT, Ganz R: On the timing of soft-tissue reconstruction for open fractures of the lower leg. *Arch Orthop Trauma Surg* 1999;119(1-2): 7-12.

19. Ostermann PA, Henry SL, Seligson D: Timing of wound closure in severe compound fractures. *Orthopedics* 1994;17(5):397-399.

20. Webb LX: New techniques in wound management: Vacuum-assisted wound closure. *J Am Acad Orthop Surg* 2002;10(5):303-311.

21. Chu CS, McManus AT, Matylevich NP, Goodwin CW, Pruitt BA Jr: Integra as a dermal replacement in a meshed composite skin graft in a rat model: A one-step operative procedure. *J Trauma* 2002;52(1):122-129.

22. De Vries HJ, Mekkes JR, Middelkoop E, Hinrichs WL, Wildevuur CR, Westerhof W: Dermal substitutes for full-thickness wounds in a one-stage grafting model. *Wound Repair Regen* 1993;1(4):244-252.

23. Wang HT, Erdmann D, Fletcher JW, Levin LS: Anterolateral thigh flap technique in hand and upper extremity reconstruction. *Tech Hand Up Extrem Surg* 2004;8(4):257-261.

24. Gopal S, Majumder S, Batchelor AG, Knight SL, De Boer P, Smith RM: Fix and flap: The radical orthopaedic and plastic treatment of severe open fractures of the tibia. *J Bone Joint Surg Br* 2000;82(7):959-966.

Chapter 5

Management of Vascular Injury in Extremity Trauma

Chih-Hung Lin, MD

Case Presentation

History

A 21-year-old man sustained a blunt abdominal contusion and a Gustilo grade IIIC open fracture of the left tibia following a high-speed motorcycle accident. He presented to the emergency department with stable vital signs. His Mangled Extremities Severity Score (MESS) was 9. Physical examination was remarkable for a large, open wound involving the left knee joint and proximal tibia with significant soft-tissue avulsions. No pulses were palpable in the injured extremity. The foot had protective sensation but virtually no motor function.

Initial Management

After evaluation by the trauma team, the patient was taken emergently to surgery, where posterior and anterior tibial artery revascularization was performed (**Figure 1**, *A*). He also underwent multiple débridements (**Figure 1**, *B*). Three weeks after wound stabilization and limb alignment with an external fixator, the patient underwent a vascularized fibula graft, which required a greater saphenous vein bypass to ensure arterial revascularization of the fibula flap from the superficial femoral artery (**Figure 1**, *C*).

Discussion

Recognizing the Problem

Lower extremity orthopaedic and vascular injuries often present with multiple trauma. Trauma patients with vascular injuries commonly sustain an overwhelming physiologic disturbance from the "lethal triad" of hemorrhagic shock, hypothermia, and acidosis. The posttraumatic systemic inflammatory response results from two factors: the first "hit" is the trauma insult, and the

Neither Dr. Lin nor any immediate family member has received anything of value from or owns stock in a commercial company or institution related directly or indirectly to the subject of this article.

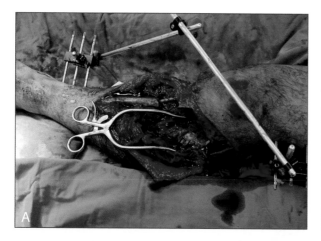

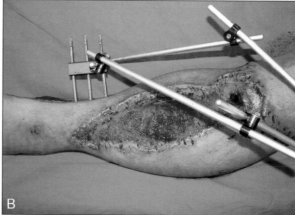

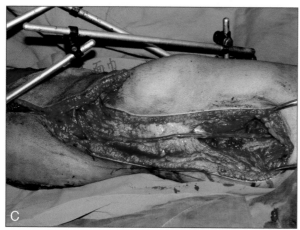

Figure 1 A 21-year-old man sustained a Gustilo IIIC open fracture of the left tibia. The patient underwent posterior and anterior tibial artery revascularization followed by fibular flap reconstruction 3 weeks after a series of four débridements. **A,** Clinical photograph shows the disruption of the anterior tibial artery, posterior tibial artery, and peroneal artery. **B,** Clinical photograph of the same composite tibial and soft-tissue defect after four débridements. **C,** Clinical photograph demonstrating the greater saphenous vein used for arterial revascularization of the fibular flap.

second "hit" is from delayed stressors, such as ischemia reperfusion injury. Early damage-control surgery and fluid resuscitation can often prevent the lethal triad. Using the damage-control surgery approach, the definitive reconstructive procedure is not performed until the overwhelming pathophysiologic inflammation has subsided. Such early damage-control techniques, developed by the military to treat battlefield injuries, are being used in civilian settings and have been found to improve outcomes in these patients.

The nature and severity of injury sustained during trauma are determined by the energy dissipated on impact. By definition, Gustilo IIIC open fractures are associated with more damage to structures than are

IIIB open fractures. They also are limb threatening and require revascularization.[1,2] Gustilo IIIC injuries are challenging to manage, especially in patients with multiple trauma and life-threatening injuries.[3-5] Delay in recognizing vascular injury or in providing optimal treatment almost always results in an unfavorable outcome. Coexisting head injury and recalcitrant exsanguinating injury to vital organs in the chest and abdomen may result in death at the scene or during transport. Patients with factors such as hypovolemic shock and head injury require emergency fluid resuscitation and timely surgical intervention, ideally in a dedicated trauma center.

Limb salvage in the setting of Gustilo IIIC open injuries requires immediate revascularization, but the severity and complexity of the damage must be assessed before surgical intervention. The reconstructive strategy should consider what the patient's ultimate function might be after the complicated reconstructive procedures have been completed. To achieve this goal, the surgeon must plan the sequence of therapeutic steps at the time of the first encounter with the patient. Failure to create and adhere to such a plan is likely to lead to eventual amputation. Several lower extremity injury severity scoring systems have been advocated to assist in the initial decision concerning limb salvage or amputation.

Scoring Systems

The most important factor influencing the possibility of limb salvage is vascular injury, which correlates with the severity of tissue ischemia. Some authors consider warm ischemia time longer than 6 hours to be an absolute indication for amputation.[6,7] An ischemic limb with blunt infrapopliteal vascular injury has the worst prognosis; under such circumstances, the amputation rate can be as high as 100%.[8,9] Even nonischemic vascular injury can have a deleterious effect on salvage attempts, however, and may lead to nonunion or infection secondary to a lack of muscular blood supply.[10,11]

Complex vascular injuries of the lower extremities caused by high-energy penetrating or blunt trauma may be associated with an unacceptably high incidence of complications, including ischemia reperfusion injury and systemic inflammatory response syndrome (SIRS). These complications often lead to limb loss. Furthermore, SIRS affects remote organs and can lead to potentially fatal multiple organ failure.[12,13] Even when a limb is salvaged, however, the multiple procedures needed to reconstruct it often leave the patient depressed, financially impoverished, and with a poorly functioning extremity. These complicating factors have led to the development of a variety of complex lower extremity injury-severity scoring systems to assist the surgeon in making the initial decision about whether to salvage or amputate a severely injured limb.

The ideal trauma limb salvage index would be 100% sensitive (all limbs with trauma limb salvage scores at or above the threshold require amputation) and 100% specific (all limbs with scores below the threshold can be salvaged), and the receiver operating characteristic curve would have an area of perfect accuracy. In fact, numerous studies have challenged the utility of all of the lower extremity injury severity scores. Bonanni and associates[14] retrospectively studied 58 severely traumatized limbs and their MESS, Limb Salvage Index (LSI), and Predictive Salvage Index (PSI) scores. They found relatively low sensitivities for the indices—the MESS had a sensitivity of 22%; the LSI 61%; and the PSI 33%—and they concluded that the indices had no predictive utility. Durham and associates[15] analyzed the MESS, LSI, and PSI results of 51 lower extremity injuries retrospectively and reported that the MESS had a sensitivity and specificity of 79% and 83%, respectively; the LSI 83% and 83%; and the PSI 96% and 50%. They found no correlation between long-term function and the severity scores. In the cohort study conducted by Bosse and associates[16] of the Lower Extremity Assessment Project (LEAP), 556 high-energy lower extremity injuries treated at eight level 1 trauma centers were prospectively evaluated using five injury-severity scoring systems for ischemic and nonischemic limbs, including the MESS; LSI; PSI; Nerve Injury, Ischemia, Soft-Tissue Injury, Skeletal Injury, Shock, and Age of Patient Score (NISSSA); and the Hannover Fracture Scale-97 (HFS-97). The sensitivity and specificity of these scoring systems were calculated. The study did not confirm the clinical usefulness of any of the lower extremity injury-severity scores, however. High scores do not always correlate with amputation, but low scores are more predictive of salvage.

These salvage scoring systems were developed in an attempt to base the initial decision-making process on more objective criteria and thereby make the decision more reliable. Although some studies mentioned above revealed both high sensitivity and specificity, the LEAP study[16] did not support the utility of any of the scoring systems for discriminating between limbs requiring amputation and those likely to be salvaged successfully. This finding suggests that, although the scores are incapable of identifying patients who will eventually require either amputation or salvage, they might still be useful as a screening test in conjunction with clinical assessment. In other words, it appears that surgeons still need to rely more on their personal clinical assessment than on scoring, which may not be accurate in all circumstances.

Ischemia Reperfusion Injury

Ischemia reperfusion injury is a common complication of multiple trauma resuscitation. Ischemia restricts the normal blood flow to tissues, thereby reducing the oxygen supply to cells and forcing them to convert to anaerobic metabolism, which is less efficient and cannot be maintained for long. Oxygen debt and cellular energy depletion lead to various biochemical alterations in the cells, including an atypical buildup of cytoplasmic metabolites and a malfunction of membrane transport systems. In the subsequent reperfusion phase, incompetent cellular membranes are exposed to a replenished intravascular supply of the calcium ion. Acting as a "second messenger," calcium triggers activation of various enzymes crucial to the production of proinflammatory mediators. Various cytokines, such as tumor necrosis factor and interleukin, are activated and, in turn, induce leukocyte sequestration. Under the influence of cytokines, cell adhesion molecules such as ICAM-1, p-selectin, and e-selectin move from the endothelium to the cytomembrane, and other cell adhesion molecules such as l-selectin and integrin move from the leukocyte to its surface. This process results in the activation of the endothelium-leukocyte interaction, with subsequent leukocyte extravasation and parenchymal tissue destruction.[17-19]

After reperfusion, excessive oxidative stress causes overwhelming leukocyte recruitment. The activation and sequestration of neutrophils also release oxygen-reactive species and proteases, further compounding the ischemia reperfusion injury. SIRS affects the bowel and generates cytokine release, which has implications for the liver, lungs, heart, brain, and kidneys.[20] This scenario represents the multiple organ dysfunction syndrome (MODS) and usually results in death.

Managing the Problem
The Damage-Control Approach

Major vascular injury can be a leading cause of hemorrhagic or ischemic morbidity in mutilating injury to the lower extremities. Most bleeding extremity trauma patients who arrive in the emergency department—especially those sustaining multiple trauma—are either hypercoagulable or coagulopathic and are frequently hypothermic. They have acidosis and hypothermia-induced coagulation factor and platelet dysfunction, combined with coagulation factor consumption, resulting in profound coagulopathy. This lethal triad of acidosis, hypothermia, and coagulopathy is associated with high morbidity and mortality. The key assumption behind the damage-control approach is that multiple-trauma patients are most likely to die of metabolic failure, characterized by the lethal triad. The principal goal of acute trauma resuscitation is to prevent the development of the lethal triad.

Damage control can be used for the staged management of severe trauma, wherein a modified surgical sequence of immediate lifesaving maneuvers is followed by physiologic stabilization and planned reoperation for definitive repair. The standard damage-control principles used for vascular injury in an extremity can be applied routinely to achieve rapid hemorrhage control and to initiate a hemostatic resuscitation plan (administering blood plasma to resuscitate a patient who has sustained a loss of blood volume due to trauma) that will correct metabolic acidosis imbalances and prevent the onset or progression of traumatic coagulopathy. The damage-control approach focuses on the rapid reversal of metabolic acidosis and the prevention of hypothermia, whereas current surgical interventions focus on controlling hemorrhage and contamination.

The "Two-Hit" Theory of Multiple Organ Failure

High-energy trauma loads induce organ and soft-tissue injuries, such as contusions or lacerations, as well as fractures. This tissue damage, along with hypoxia and hypotension, triggers local and systemic host responses (resulting in SIRS) designed to preserve immune system integrity and stimulate reparative mechanisms.[21,22] The body's initial response to traumatic injury includes the activation of proinflammatory cytokines, complement factors, coagulation systems, acute phase proteins, neuroendocrine mediators, and an accumulation of immunocompetent cells from the local site of tissue damage, which inflict a systemic inflammatory reaction or apoptosis on the cells of distant visceral organs.

The initial systemic inflammation from the first insult is augmented by a delayed second "hit" from such stressors as ischemia reperfusion injury, respiratory distress, metabolic acidosis, necrotic tissue, surgical interventions, or infection. Although the first physiologic insult alone might not be sufficient to induce multiple organ failure, the additional assault of the second hit could be. This model is known as the "two-hit" theory of multiple organ dysfunction.[23]

Inappropriate surgical intervention or intensive care unit management can exacerbate the second hit. Vascular injuries of the extremities with accompanying hemorrhagic shock sustain tissue ischemic insult. After fluid resuscitation and revascularization, the compromised vascular tissue can develop reperfusion injury. Severe muscle crush injury and rhabdomyolysis, as well as ischemia reperfusion injury, predispose to compartment syndrome, inflammatory activity, and infection. The local and systemic release of proinflammatory cytokines, free radicals, and phospholipids activates the recruitment of leukocyte sequestration and infiltration, inducing a complex, imbalanced host defense response. This overwhelming proinflammatory storm leads to the clinical manifestation of SIRS and finally to host defense failure with resulting multiple organ failure.

Although most patients with lower limb injuries do not present with hemodynamic instability, those who do have a significant risk of systemic morbidities because of the likelihood that their physiologic reserves will be depleted. The accompanying visceral organ damage typically includes not only pulmonary damage, but also damage to the brain, liver, and kidneys. Rhabdomyolysis often is accompanied by acute renal failure, and temporary hemodialysis may be needed. Seekamp and associates[5] reported on patients with IIIC open fractures of the lower extremities requiring immediate amputation, secondary amputation after a limb salvage procedure, or limb salvage. The authors found that patients in all three groups sustained respiratory insufficiency and required ventilator treatment for an average of more than 10 days.

Traumatic Shock Management

"Traumatic shock" has been conceptualized as an independent postinflammatory state secondary to immune activation (SIRS) by the inflammatory cascade superimposed on the trauma itself, although this phenomenon is likely indistinguishable from the organ dysfunction seen after fluid resuscitation for severe injury or illness.[24,25] In the setting of traumatic shock, a loss of vasomotor tone will be present. Mahoney and associates[26] reported that the specific etiology of shock following blunt trauma injury is due to hypovolemia in 59% of cases, to isolated head injuries in 16% of cases, to "other" causes (predominantly obstructive) in 13% of cases, to neurogenic causes in 7% of cases, and to injuries too complex to adequately classify in 5% of cases.

The treatment of traumatic shock requires attention to its primary causes and prompt hemorrhage control and repayment of the oxygen debt. Only then can attention be turned to the débridement of necrotic tissue, the stabilization of bony injuries, and the treatment of soft-tissue wounds as appropriate.

Hemorrhage is not the only cause of posttraumatic shock in multiple-trauma patients, but it is the most prevalent cause in vascular injuries of the extremities. Hemorrhagic shock marked by hypotension is rarely seen in patients with less than a 30% blood-volume deficit, and it indicates an advanced state of physiologic exhaustion.[27] Hemorrhage control is much more important than fluid resuscitation, and hemorrhage mandates the earliest possible definitive management.[27]

Unstable patients nearing physiologic exhaustion require abbreviated, or "damage-control," surgical tactics. This need should be recognized early in the resuscitation rather than later, during a surgical procedure, such as a limb amputation. In the management of hemorrhagic shock, liberal amounts of crystalloid solutions and packed red blood cells (PRBCs) are used, but large-volume infusions in the setting of a major hemorrhage set the stage for the lethal triad.[12,13,28-31] Recent experience with patients with massive hemorrhage in both civilian and military settings supports early volume resuscitation with generous plasma at a ratio of 1:1, using PRBCs or plasma as the primary resuscitation fluid.[32] The survival of unstable multiple-trauma patients can be improved by the early correction of these physiologic derangements. Future advances in trauma resuscitation from hypovolemic shock may involve the use of procoagulant medications, imaging technology, circulatory assist techniques, and inflammatory modulators.[33]

Deciding Against Limb Salvage

Because of pathophysiologic exhaustion, attempts at limb salvage may result in multiple organ dysfunction and a lethal outcome, despite secondary amputation. Once the systemic response has progressed to the point of organ dysfunction, amputation will not halt the systemic response.[5] Despite improved surgical techniques and intensive care, therefore, amputation still has to be considered as a therapeutic option in severe open fractures with vascular injury and accompanying multiple trauma, and the decision to discontinue limb salvage should be made early and be based not only on the condition of the traumatized limb but also on the systemic physiologic presentation.[34,35]

CT Angiography

The clinical signs of a vascular injury can be divided into hard criteria (eg, absence of a pulse) and soft criteria (eg, suspected vascular injury with limb perfusion evident). If hard criteria are present, physical examination is the most expeditious and accurate way of determining the presence of an arterial injury, with accuracy exceeding 95%.[36,37] Physical examination, however, cannot reliably exclude a vascular injury, especially in an unstable patient.[38,39] Traditional angiography is time-consuming, making it infeasible for the evaluation of extremity vascular injury in the unstable patient. Multidetector fine-resolution CT angiography, however, provides not only a total-body trauma survey, but also accurate and timely diagnosis of peripheral vascular injuries.[40] Using multidetector CT angiography with two-dimensional reformation and three-dimensional rendering allows visualization of injury to the bone, muscle, and vasculature. Thus, CT angiography is our initial diagnostic modality of choice in the initial evaluation of arterial injury.[41] It provides an informative study for surgical intervention and can guide nonsurgical management when appropriate in patients who require damage-control surgery and resuscitation.

Compartment Syndrome

When the major artery of a limb is disrupted and subsequently repaired during damage-control surgery, an adjunctive open fasciotomy is often the best course, because critical limb ischemia or early compartment syndrome is difficult to diagnose in the immediate postoperative period.[42-44] After revascularization, the subsequent reperfusion injury will provoke an overwhelming release of cytokines and free radicals. This second "hit" carries the risk of multiple organ damage.

Compartment syndrome also has been linked to vascular compromise after the restoration of blood flow and is a major risk factor for limb loss after any limb salvage procedure. Fasciotomy should always be performed in a coagulopathic patient because a closed soft-tissue envelope may result in a compartment hematoma, and the edematous skin and muscle itself may be a source of constriction, elevating intracompartmental pressures. In the event of high-energy damage, the avulsed distal muscle will be nonfunctional and should be excised to minimize complications associated with muscle necrosis and wound sepsis.[45] In addition, the reduced volume of the ischemic lower extremity muscle is beneficial in minimizing compartmental pressure after revascularization.

Soft-Tissue Coverage Using Free Flaps

Data collected as part of a multicenter, prospective outcome study of 601 patients with high-energy lower extremity injuries in the LEAP project[16] show that soft-tissue injury severity has the greatest impact on whether to salvage a limb. Several factors have been associated with the risk of limb loss after lower extremity trauma, including infection, chronic pain, and nonunion. The eventual outcome of a compound fracture of the tibia depends not on the radiologic appearance of the excellence of the reduction of the bone, but on the viability and condition of the surrounding soft tissue. Early free-tissue transfer provides well-vascularized tissue coverage to protect the open wound from the additional loss of soft tissue and bone by desiccation.[46,47] Delays in obtaining coverage after significant soft-tissue injury have been associated with an increased risk of infection, with or without nonunion, and eventual amputation.[46] With the advent of dressings such as vacuum-assisted closure, the exposed soft tissue and bone can be covered temporarily, until regularly scheduled reconstructive procedures can be performed.[48]

Yaremchuk and associates[49] recommended muscle flap closure at 7 to 14 days after injury if the neurovascular structures have been protected, because of the common difficulty in accurately defining the zone of soft-tissue injury caused by high-energy trauma. Additionally, recovery from multisystem trauma is responsible for long delays in some patients,[49] and 10% to 17% of patients with massively mangled lower extremities have an associated life-threatening injury,[50] which clearly would take priority over wound coverage. Pape and associates[51] performed a prospective study that showed the inflammatory response in multiple-trauma patients who underwent secondary definitive surgery at days 2 to 4 was significantly higher than in those who underwent surgery at days 6 to 8. Several experimental and clinical studies have demonstrated that use of the damage-control surgery concept can reduce the resulting inflammatory response, leading to an improved clinical outcome after physiologic status has stabilized.[52] Given this evidence, early major surgery has to be judged too great a burden for the patient with both orthopaedic and vascular injuries, especially those with multiple trauma. Major surgical procedures at days 2 to 4 should be avoided. The definitive reconstructive free-tissue transfer surgery is often more appropriately done 1 week after trauma, when the inflammatory response has calmed down.

Case Management and Outcome Summary

Bony union occurred 11 months following the free tissue transfer, and the patient had excellent sensation and functional range of motion of the ankle (Figure 2).

Because of the significant crush injury and the precarious nature of the vessel repair, a determination of the soft-tissue and bony defects could not be made until the sequential débridements had been completed and a period of time had passed. The priority in such cases is to let the vascular repairs mature before any extensive reconstructive surgery is undertaken. In most cases, early coverage in wound closure is desirable, but cases such as this require a slow approach to wound care that emphasizes trauma resuscitation, vascular repair, and healing before bony repair can be

undertaken, to prevent the onset of the lethal triad of acidosis, hypothermia, and coagulopathy.

The importance of this case lies in its demonstration of the need to first manage the Gustilo IIIC injury using techniques from trauma surgery and vascular surgery. Such IIIC injuries usually require macrovascular techniques, such as direct vessel repair after mobilization or short interposition vein grafts, which are characteristically done by vascular surgeons. The microvascular or replantation surgeon may be called to use the operating microscope to facilitate accurate interposition vein replacement more distally on the extremity. Recognizing the presence of a vascular injury and repairing as many interrupted vessels as possible can improve the ability of the bone and other soft tissues to heal.

If a second free-tissue transfer is required, one of the vessels in the leg may have to be used as an end artery, although many microvascular extremity surgeons perform end-to-side anastomoses or interposition vein grafts (as was done in this case) for more proximal vessels to avoid further vascular impairment of the limb by robbing the blood supply from a dominant or repaired vessel.

Strategies for Minimizing Common Complications

Various lower extremity injury severity scoring systems allow an emergent assessment of the appropriateness of limb salvage. Recent advances in patient-specific trauma care—such as the acceptance of damage-control procedures and the use of multidetector CT angiography in the multiple-trauma patient with orthopaedic and vascular injuries—favor early damage-control resuscitation that can minimize the biological first hit of traumatic injury. Only after the second hit has been managed can an appropriate reconstructive strategy for limb salvage become possible.

References

1. Punch J, Rees R, Cashmer B, Oldham K, Wilkins E, Smith DJ Jr: Acute lung injury following reperfusion after ischemia in the hind limbs of rats. *J Trauma* 1991;31:760-767.

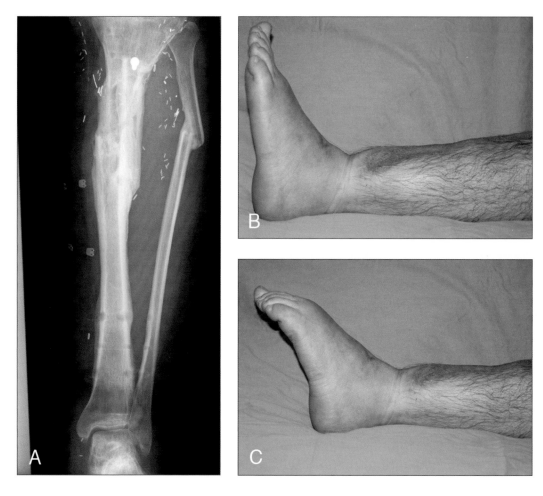

Figure 2 Postoperative images of the leg of the 21-year-old man described in the case presentation at 11-month follow-up. **A,** AP radiograph view demonstrating bone union after 11 months. Clinical photographs showing ankle dorsiflexion (**B**) and plantar flexion (**C**) in the same patient.

2. Klausner JM, Anner H, Paterson IS, et al: Lower torso ischemia-induced lung injury is leukocyte dependent. *Ann Surg* 1988;208:761-767.

3. Tassiopoulos AK, Carlin RE, Gao Y, et al: Role of nitric oxide and tumor necrosis factor on lung injury caused by ischemia/reperfusion of the lower extremities. *J Vasc Surg* 1997;26:647-656.

4. Lin CH, Wei FC, Levin SL, Su JI, Yeh WL: The functional outcome of lower-extremity fractures with vascular injury. *J Trauma* 1997;43:480-485.

5. Seekamp A, Regel G, Hildebrand F, Sander J, Tscherne H: Parameters of multiple organ dysfunction fail to predict secondary amputation following limb salvage in multiply traumatized patients. *Injury* 1999;30:199-207.

6. Moniz MP, Ombrellaro MP, Stevens SL, Freeman MB, Diamond DL, Goldman MH: Concomitant orthopedic and vascular injuries predictors for limb loss in blunt lower extremity trauma. *Am Surg* 1997;63:24-28.

7. Lange RH, Bach AW, Hansen ST Jr, Johansen KH: Open tibial fractures with associated vascular injuries: Prognosis for limb salvage. *J Trauma* 1985;25:203-208.

8. Lazarides MK, Arvanitis DP, Kopadis GC, Tsoupanos SS, Dayantas JN: Popliteal artery and trifurcation injuries: Is it possible to predict the outcome? *Eur J Vasc Surg* 1994;8:226-230.

9. Padberg FT Jr, Rubelowsky JJ, Hernandez-Maldonado JJ, et al: Infrapopliteal arterial injury: Prompt revascularization affords optimal limb salvage. *J Vasc Surg* 1992;16:877-886.

10. Purry NA, Hannon MA: How successful is below-knee amputation for injury? *Injury* 1989;20:32-36.

11. Scalea TM, Mann R, Austin R, Herschowitz M: Staged procedures for exsanguinating lower extremity trauma: An extension of a technique. Case report. *J Trauma* 1994;36:291-293.

12. Holcomb JB, Jenkins D, Rhee P, et al: Damage control resuscitation: Directly addressing the early coagulopathy of trauma. *J Trauma* 2007;62:307-310.

13. Hess JR, Holcomb JB, Hoyt DB: Damage control resuscitation: The need for specific blood products to treat the coagulopathy of trauma. *Transfusion* 2006;46:685-686.

14. Bonanni F, Rhodes M, Lucke JF: The futility of predictive scoring of mangled lower extremities. *J Trauma* 1993;34:99-104.

15. Durham RM, Mistry BM, Mazuski JE, Shapiro M, Jacobs D: Outcome and utility of scoring systems in the management of the mangled extremity. *Am J Surg* 1996;172:569-574.

16. Bosse MJ, MacKenzie EJ, Kellam JF, Burgess AR, Webb LX: A prospective evaluation of the clinical utility of the lower extremity injury-severity scores. *J Bone Joint Surg Am* 2001;83:3-14.

17. Kokura S, Yoshida N, Yoshikawa T: Anoxia/reoxygenation-induced leukocyte-endothelial cell interactions. *Free Radic Biol Med* 2002;33:427-432.

18. Becker LB: New concepts in reactive oxygen species and cardiovascular reperfusion physiology. *Cardiovasc Res* 2004;61:461-470.

19. Russell RC, Roth AC, Kucan JO, Zook EG: Reperfusion injury and oxygen free radicals: A review. *J Reconstr Microsurg* 1989;5:79-84.

20. Harkin DW, Barros D'sa AA, McCallion K, Hoper M, Halliday MI, Campbell FC: Circulating neutrophil priming and systemic inflammation in limb ischaemia-reperfusion injury. *Int Angiol* 2001;20:78-89.

21. Rotstein OD: Modeling the two-hit hypothesis for evaluating strategies to prevent organ injury after shock/resuscitation. *J Trauma* 2003;54:S203-S206.

22. Kluger Y, Gonze MD, Paul DB, et al: Blunt vascular injury associated with closed mid-shaft femur fracture: A plea for concern. *J Trauma* 1994;36:222-225.

23. Keel M, Trentz O: Pathophysiology of polytrauma. *Injury* 2005;36:691-709.

24. Harbrecht BG, Alarcron LH, Peitzman AB: Management of shock, in Moore EE, Feliciano DV, Mattox KL (eds): *Trauma*, ed 5. New York, NY, McGraw-Hill, 2004, pp 201-226.

25. Peitzman AB, Billiar TR, Harbrecht BG, Kelly E, Udekwu AO, Simmons RL: Hemorrhagic shock. *Curr Probl Surg* 1995;32:925-1002.

26. Mahoney EJ, Biffl WL, Harrington DT, Cioffi WG: Isolated brain injury as a cause of hypotension in the blunt trauma patient. *J Trauma* 2003;55:1065-1069.

27. American College of Surgeons Committee on Trauma: *Advanced Trauma Life Support Course for Doctors: Instructor Course Manual.* Chicago, IL, American College of Surgeons, 2004.

28. Moore FA, McKinley BA, Moore EE: The next generation in shock resuscitation. *Lancet* 2004;363:1988-1996.

29. Tieu BH, Holcomb JB, Schreiber MA: Coagulopathy: Its pathophysiology and treatment in the injured patient. *World J Surg* 2007;31:1055-1064.

30. Kauvar DS, Holcomb JB, Norris GC, Hess JR: Fresh whole blood transfusion: A controversial military practice. *J Trauma* 2006;61:181-184.

31. Malone DL, Hess JR, Fingerhut A: Massive transfusion practices around the globe and a suggestion for a common massive transfusion protocol. *J Trauma* 2006;60:S91-S96.

32. Borgman MA, Spinella PC, Perkins JG, et al: The ratio of blood products transfused affects mortality in patients receiving massive transfusions at a combat support hospital. *J Trauma* 2007;63:805-813.

33. Kirkpatrick AW, Ball CG, D'Amours SK, Zygun D: Acute resuscitation of the unstable adult trauma patient: Bedside diagnosis and therapy. *Can J Surg* 2008;51:57-69.

34. Rotondo MF, Schwab CW, McGonigal MD, et al: 'Damage control': An approach for improved survival in exsanguinating penetrating abdominal injury. *J Trauma* 1993;35:375-383.

35. Burch JM, Ortiz VB, Richardson RJ, Martin RR, Mattox KL, Jordan GL Jr: Abbreviated laparotomy and planned reoperation for critically injured patients. *Ann Surg* 1992;215:476-484.

36. Frykberg ER, Dennis JW, Bishop K, Laneve L, Alexander RH: The reliability of physical examination in the evaluation of penetrating extremity trauma for vascular injury: Results at one year. *J Trauma* 1991;31:502-511.

37. Frykberg ER, Crump JM, Vines FS, et al: A reassessment of the role of arteriography in penetrating proximity extremity trauma: A prospective study. *J Trauma* 1989;29:1041-1052.

38. McCormick TM, Burch BH: Routine angiographic evaluation of neck and extremity injuries. *J Trauma* 1979;19:384-387.

39. Norman J, Gahtan V, Franz M, Bramson R: Occult vascular injuries following gunshot wounds resulting in long bone fractures of the extremities. *Am Surg* 1995;61:146-150.

40. Peng PD, Spain DA, Tataria M, Hellinger JC, Rubin GD, Brundage SI: CT angiography effectively evaluates extremity vascular trauma. *Am Surg* 2008;74:103-107.

41. Fishman EK, Horton KM, Johnson PT: Multidetector CT and three-dimensional CT angiography for suspected vascular trauma of the extremities. *Radiographics* 2008;28:653-666.

42. Fields CK, Senkowsky J, Hollier LH, et al: Fasciotomy in vascular trauma: Is it too much, too often? *Am Surg* 1994;60:409-411.

43. Fainzilber G, Roy-Shapira A, Wall MJ Jr, Mattox KL: Predictors of amputation for popliteal artery injuries. *Am J Surg* 1995;170:568-571.

44. Patman RD, Thompson JE: Fasciotomy in peripheral vascular surgery: Report of 164 patients. *Arch Surg* 1970;101:663-672.

45. Chuang DC, Lai JB, Cheng SJ, Jain V, Lin CH, Chen HC: Traction avulsion amputation of the major upper limb: A proposed new classification, guidelines for acute management, and strategies for secondary reconstruction. *Plast Reconstr Surg* 2001;108:1624-1638.

46. Godina M: Early microsurgical reconstruction of complex trauma of the extremities. *Plast Reconstr Surg* 1986;78:285-292.

47. Byrd HS, Cierny G III, Tebbetts JB: The management of open tibial fracture with associated soft tissue loss: External pin fixation with early flap coverage. *Plast Reconst Surg* 1981;68:73-82.

48. Bhattacharyya T, Mehta P, Smith M, Pomahac B: Routine use of wound vacuum-assisted closure does not allow coverage delay for open tibia fractures. *Plast Reconstr Surg* 2008;121:1263-1266.

49. Yaremchuk MJ, Brumback RJ, Manson PN, Burgess AR, Poka A, Weiland AJ: Acute and definitive management of traumatic osteocutaneous defects of the lower extremity. *Plast Reconstr Surg* 1987;80:1-14.

50. McAndrew MP, Lantz BA: Initial care of massively traumatized lower extremity. *Clin Orthop Relat Res* 1989;243:20-29.

51. Pape HC, van Griensven M, Rice J, et al: Major secondary surgery in blunt trauma patients and perioperative cytokine liberation: Determination of the clinical relevance of biochemical markers. *J Trauma* 2001;50:989-1000.

52. Hildebrand F, Giannoudis P, Krettek C, Pape HC: Damage control: Extremities. *Injury* 2004;35:678-689.

Chapter 6

Malunions and Nonunions in the Lower Extremity

Salih Marangoz, MD
Janet D. Conway, MD
John E. Herzenberg, MD, FRCSC

Case Presentation
History

A 44-year-old woman sustained a grade II Gustilo open fracture after being struck by a vehicle while walking. Her medical history was significant for schizophrenia and smoking. Initial treatment consisted of an intramedullary rod with a small anti-kick plate on the anterior aspect of the tibia. The fracture did not heal, however, and the intramedullary rod began to bend. The rod subsequently was removed and a lateral plating was performed. The patient presented at our clinic 1 year later with pain at the nonunion site and a valgus deformity.

Current Problem

On physical examination, the patient had good range of motion of the knee and ankle. The thigh-foot axis was 15° external with no rotational deformity. The skin was intact without any evidence of draining sinuses or infection. A prominence was present under the skin at the level of the nonunion, which was consistent with the mobile nonunion and broken plate. Her pulse was +2 and sensation was intact. When manually stressed, the nonunion site displayed about 10° of motion. During surgery, however, once the fibula was osteotomized, the mobility of the tibial nonunion increased to 20°.

Radiographic evaluation included a weight-bearing AP view of both legs from the hips to the ankles (**Figure 1**, *A*) and a lateral long-leg view of the left leg (**Figure 1**, *B*). Deformity analysis of the radiographs demonstrated a posterior proximal tibial angle (PPTA) of 72°, a medial proximal tibial angle (MPTA) of 96°, and a lateral mechanical axis deviation of 15 mm. These measurements confirmed the procurvatum and valgus deformity. The radiographs

Dr. Conway or an immediate family member has received research or institutional support from Medtronic and Synthes and is a consultant for or an employee of Smith & Nephew. Dr. Herzenberg or an immediate family member has received research or institutional support from Smith & Nephew and Orthofix. Neither Dr. Marangoz nor any immediate family member has received anything of value from or owns stock in a commercial company or institution related directly or indirectly to the subject of this article.

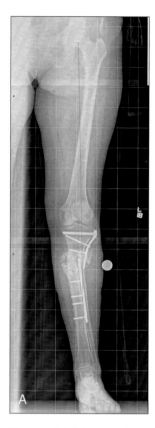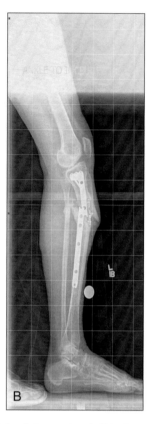

Figure 1 Mal-nonunion of the left proximal tibia in a 44-year-old woman. AP weight-bearing radiograph (**A**) and lateral radiograph (**B**) views demonstrate the tibia valga and procurvatum deformity of the proximal tibia with failed lateral plate fixation. (Reproduced with permission from the Rubin Institute for Advanced Orthopedics, Sinai Hospital of Baltimore, copyright 2009.)

also showed a very small retained antikick plate, a lateral broken plate, and an atrophic nonunion of the proximal tibia.

DISCUSSION
Recognizing Malunions and Nonunions and High-Risk Situations

Many factors can compromise the healing of open fractures. Local patient factors include soft-tissue injury, periosteal stripping, infection, and vascular injury. General patient factors, such as age, underlying medical conditions, and smoking, along with inadequate (unstable) fixation of a fracture also may contribute.[1] These factors can lead to a high incidence of delayed union and nonunion.

Malunion

Malunions are characterized by at least one of the following components: angulation, translation, rotation, or shortening. The desired result of fracture treatment is bony union with normal alignment. Union with unacceptable angulation or translation in the frontal, sagittal, or axial plane is called malunion. Malunion can lead to functional disability, poor cosmesis, or joint malalignment.[2] Malunion alters the forces on adjacent joints and can contribute to early degenerative arthritis, although the precise threshold in degrees of deformity is open to debate.[3-7] The level and magnitude of the malunion correlates with any subsequent osteoarthritis.

Malunion can result from physician factors or patient factors. Physician factors include inaccurate initial reduction and inadequate fixation. Immobilization of an unstable fracture with a cast is an example of inadequate fixation. Patient factors include noncompliance (eg, failure to comply with restricted weight bearing) and the presence of underlying adverse medical or physiologic issues.

A malunited fracture in a child may remodel if it is close to a growth plate, has sufficient growth-remaining potential, and lies in the plane of joint motion (eg, procurvatum or recurvatum around the knee joint). Fractures in adults have negligible remodeling potential and thus are more prone to functional limitations and early degenerative arthritis.

Nonunion

Nonunion occurs when a fractured bone does not heal in an expected period of time, which is defined variably. Some surgeons define this period as being between 3 months and 8 months from the time of injury.[8] The US Food and Drug Administration (FDA) defines nonunion as "established when bone has not healed completely within a minimum of 9 months from the injury and the fracture has not shown progressive signs of healing over 3 consecutive months on serial radiographs."[9,10] Radiologically, nonunion is diagnosed by the absence of bridging trabeculae on plain radiographs, along with pain at the site. CT can help to visualize the irregular internal geometry of the nonunion.[11] A technetium Tc 99m bone scan will show increased uptake at the site of a nonunion, except in atrophic or avascular nonunions.[8]

Etiology of Nonunion

Nonunion is more common in open fractures than in closed fractures because of the high energy of the injury and the vascular compromise secondary to periosteal stripping.[12] Factors leading to nonunion include inadequate fracture stabilization, excessive interfragmental gap, vascular compromise, infection, and patient factors such as smoking and diabetes.

Classifications of Nonunions

Weber, and Ĉech[13] differentiated two main types of nonunions: viable (hypertrophic or hypervascular) and nonviable (atrophic or avascular). Viable nonunions, although dormant, have the potential to become biologically active for healing, whereas nonviable nonunions do not.

Nonunions can be described from a mobility perspective.[14] Nonunions with less than 5° of motion are called nonmobile or stiff. Most stiff nonunions are hypertrophic. Those with moderate mobility, between 5° and 20° in one plane, are called partly mobile or lax. Nonunions with more than 20° of motion in multiple planes are called mobile or flail. Most flail nonunions are atrophic, although they could be oligotrophic. The stiffness of a nonunion is an indirect reflection of the type of tissue that exists between the nonunited bone ends. The stiffer the nonunion, the more likely that dense, fibrous, fibrocartilaginous tissue is present in the nonunion region; this type of tissue can be transformed into bone using distraction osteogenesis techniques.[15]

The drawback of classifying nonunions according to mobility is the difficulty in characterizing the true mobility at the nonunion site, especially in the presence of an internal fixation, an intact fibula, or a juxta-articular nonunion. A mobile atrophic nonunion of the tibia might not be assessed adequately until the fibula is osteotomized (**Figure 2**). Sometimes it is necessary to remove the internal fix-

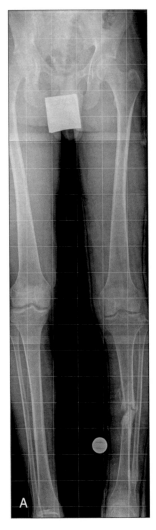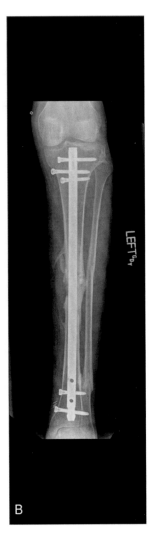

Figure 2 Atrophic varus mal-nonunion (malaligned nonunion) of the tibia in a 25-year-old man. **A,** Weight-bearing AP view demonstrates a mal-nonunion in the left tibia. **B,** AP view shows the same patient after treatment with intramedullary nailing and an autologous bone graft. (Reproduced with permission from the Rubin Institute for Advanced Orthopedics, Sinai Hospital of Baltimore, copyright 2009.)

ation, cut the fibula, and do a fluoroscopic examination of the nonunion site to differentiate the nonunion motion from the joint motion.

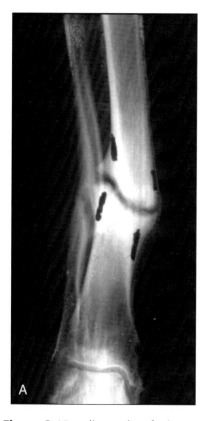
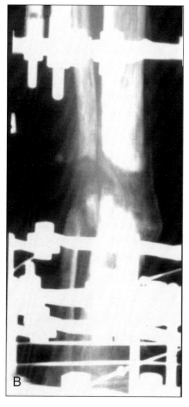
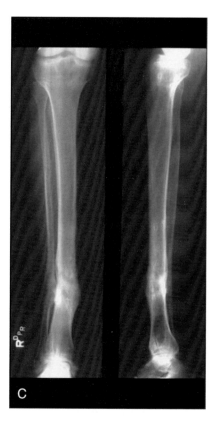

Figure 3 AP radiographs of a hypertrophic mal-nonunion in valgus. **A,** The mal-nonunion resulted in a 2-cm limb-length discrepancy. **B,** The deformity was treated by gradual distraction through the nonunion with an Ilizarov fixator. **C,** Final healing, realignment, and length restoration were achieved. (Reproduced with permission from the Rubin Institute for Advanced Orthopedics, Sinai Hospital of Baltimore, copyright 2009.)

We recommend using one of the following treatment techniques, once the mobility of the nonunion has been established. For stiff nonunions, we distract the nonunion site. For partly mobile nonunions, we first compress the nonunion site for 1 week and then distract it using Ilizarov principles, to obtain distraction osteogenesis. Compression should be done gradually over 1 week at a rate of 1 mm/day, followed by a gradual distraction at a rate of 0.5 mm/day. The initial compression helps to stimulate osteogenesis if the fibrous tissue is less stiff.[15,16] If the nonunion is truly mobile, then the best treatment is bone grafting and stabilization of the nonunion site.

Mal-nonunion

Nonunions can be aligned or malaligned. Malaligned nonunions can be termed "mal-nonunions."[15] The dual objectives for the treatment of mal-nonunions are to correct the deformity and to achieve healing of the nonunion.[8] Uniting the bone ends in the presence of unacceptable angulation, rotation, or shortening is unwise.

Mal-nonunions can be stiff or flail, depending on the structure of the tissues between the bone ends.[15] Stiff mal-nonunions are hypertrophic, indicating that fibrocartilaginous tissue is present at the nonunion site. This type of mal-nonunion can be corrected gradually using distraction techniques that do not require opening the nonunion site[17] (**Figure 3**). For flail mal-nonunions, other strategies are required, such as open grafting or realignment with internal or external fixation.[15] In certain partly mobile mal-nonunions, the nonunion can be stimulated to heal by initial compression for a few weeks, followed by gradual distraction to correct the malalignment.

Managing Malunions and Nonunions

Deformity Analysis

Posttraumatic malunion deformity should be evaluated radiographically with weight-bearing AP and lateral long-leg views taken with a lift under the shorter leg. Deformity analysis begins with the malalignment and malorientation tests.[18]

Malalignment Test

For the malalignment test, the centers of the femoral head and ankle are marked on the weight-bearing AP view and a line connecting these two points is drawn. This line defines the mechanical axis of the entire leg. The distance from the center of the knee to that line is the mechanical axis deviation. The mechanical axis normally should be 0 mm to 8 mm medial to the center of the knee joint. This test will define overall varus or valgus malalignment.

Next, a condylar line is drawn tangential to the distal femoral condyles (the distal femoral joint orientation line) and tibial plateau (the proximal tibial joint

orientation line). Another line is drawn from the center of the femoral head to the center of the knee joint to describe the mechanical axis of the femur. The intersection of this line with the condylar line forms the mechanical lateral distal femoral angle (mLDFA). The normal mean value of the mLDFA is 88° (range, 85° to 90°). A line is then drawn from the center of the knee joint to the center of the ankle, to form the mechanical axis of the tibia. The intersection of this line with a tibial plateau line drawn across the tibial plateau forms the medial proximal tibial angle (MPTA). The normal mean value of this angle is 87° (range, 85° to 90°). A value that is out of range indicates which bone (the femur, tibia, or both) is contributing to the mechanical axis deviation (**Figure 4, *A***).

The last step of the malalignment test measures the joint-line convergence angle, which is the angle between the femoral condylar and tibial plateau lines. This angle usually is less than 3°. Angles greater than 3° point to knee-joint laxity as the source of the mechanical axis deviation. To evaluate ankle and hip alignment, however, separate malorientation tests should be performed.

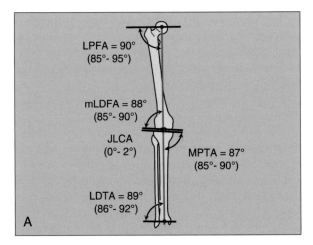

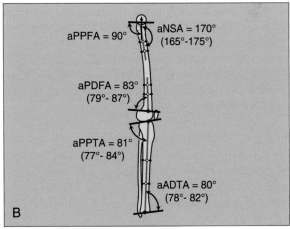

Figure 4 Schematics showing deformity analysis parameters for the malalignment and malorientation tests. **A,** Frontal plane joint orientation angles are shown, relative to the mechanical axis lines. **B,** Sagittal plane joint orientation angles are demonstrated. LPFA = lateral proximal femoral angle, mLDFA = mechanical lateral distal femoral angle, JLCA = joint line convergence angle, MPTA = medial proximal tibial angle, LDTA = lateral distal tibial angle, aNSA = anatomic neck-shaft angle, aPPFA = anatomic posterior proximal femoral angle, aPDFA = anatomic posterior distal femoral angle, aPPTA = anatomic posterior proximal tibial angle, aADTA = anatomic anterior distal tibial angle. (Reproduced with permission from Paley D: Normal lower limb alignment and joint orientation, in Herzenberg JE, ed: *Principles of Deformity Correction*, ed 3. New York, NY, Springer Verlag, 2005, pp 1-18.)

Malorientation Test

For the malorientation test, one line is drawn from the center of the femoral head tangential to the greater trochanter (the trochanter-head line or hip-joint orientation line), and another line is drawn across the tibial plafond tangential to the ankle joint. The angle formed on the lateral side of the tibia's mechanical axis at the ankle joint line is called the lateral distal tibial angle (LDTA). The normal mean value of this angle is 89° (range, 86° to 92°). The angle between the hip-joint orientation line and the mechanical axis of the femur is called the mechanical lateral proximal femoral angle (mLPFA). Its normal value is 90° (range, 85° to 95°) (**Figure 4, A**).

Measurement of the sagittal angles is done on lateral radiographs (**Figure 4, B**). The sagittal distal femoral joint line is drawn through the physeal scar in adults, and through the growth plate in children. The sagittal proximal tibial joint line is drawn tangential to the tibial plateau on the sagittal plane. Mid-diaphyseal lines are drawn through the tibia and the distal femur. The mid-diaphyseal line of the femur intersects the femoral joint line one third of the distance from its most anterior point to form the posterior distal femoral angle (PDFA). The mid-diaphyseal line of the tibia intersects the proximal tibia joint line one fifth of the distance from its most anterior point to form the posterior proximal tibial angle (PPTA). The normal value for the PDFA is 83° (range, 79° to 87°). The normal value for the PPTA is 81° (range, 77° to 84°) (**Figure 4, B**).

Center of Rotation of Angulation

The malorientation and malalignment tests indicate which bone is causing the problem. The next goal is to find the apex of the deformity, also known as the center of rotation of angulation (CORA). CORA analysis helps the surgeon to identify the theoretically ideal site for deformity correction. CORA analysis can be performed according to anatomic or mechanical axis planning.[19] Frontal and sagittal plane analyses will reveal where in the bone segment (eg, tibia, femur) the CORA is located. It is beyond the scope of this chapter to describe the intricacies of deformity analysis planning, which is described in standard texts.[20] It is possible for more than one CORA to be present. If only one CORA exists in either one of these planes, then the abnormality is a simple uniapi-cal deformity in the frontal or sagittal plane. If more than one CORA is present in any of these planes, then a multiapical deformity is present. For most fracture malunions, the deformity lies neither solely in the AP nor in the lateral plane, but instead in a nonanatomic oblique plane.[21] The magnitude and orientation of the oblique plane can be analyzed accurately using the graphic method for most deformities less than 45° in magnitude.[22]

Treatment Options for Malunions

Osteotomy

Typical problems that need correction, in addition to the malunion itself, include adjacent stiff joints and limb-length discrepancy (actual or secondary to malunion). The preferred treatment for correction of a malunion is an osteotomy. A CORA analysis along with a basic understanding of osteotomy principles will help the surgeon make the best decisions about osteotomy type and level. The ideal level at which to perform an osteotomy is at the level of the CORA. That level may be an undesirable biologic site, however, because of sclerotic bone or a poor skin envelope. The most important osteotomy principle to understand is that an angular osteotomy done at a level above or below the CORA requires compensatory translation along with the angulation to maintain proper alignment of the limb.[20]

Many malunions produce translational as well as angular deformity, sometimes in different planes. Green and Gibbs[21] showed that very few malunion deformities actually occur in the standard anatomic frontal or sagittal planes; instead, they most often occur in oblique planes. Osteotomy above or below the CORA might straighten the bone, but it also could leave a bump at the deformity site. Performing osteotomy through the old fracture site could help to prevent a bump, but this site could be compromised biologically in terms of healing or soft-tissue coverage.

Joints adjacent to the deformity can become stiff after trauma and any subsequent cast immobilization. Aggressive physical therapy or surgical release might be necessary adjunct treatments. Stiff joints increase the lever arm on the nonunion/malunion fixation. This condition is seen most commonly in distal tibial recurvatum nonunions, which often are

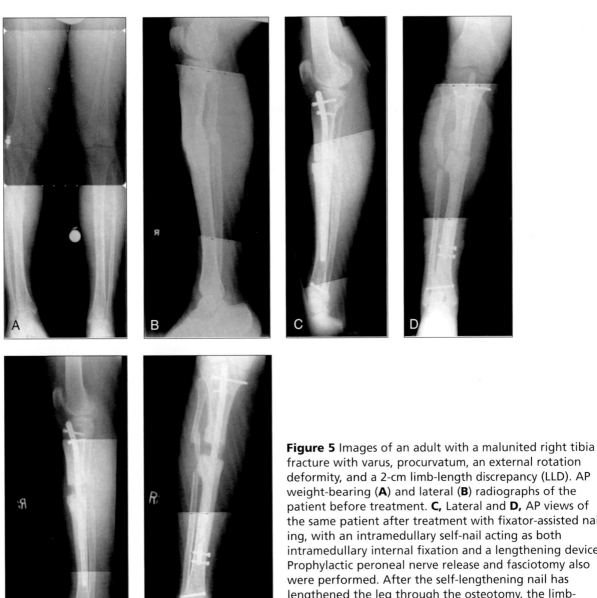

Figure 5 Images of an adult with a malunited right tibia fracture with varus, procurvatum, an external rotation deformity, and a 2-cm limb-length discrepancy (LLD). AP weight-bearing (**A**) and lateral (**B**) radiographs of the patient before treatment. **C,** Lateral and **D,** AP views of the same patient after treatment with fixator-assisted nailing, with an intramedullary self-nail acting as both intramedullary internal fixation and a lengthening device. Prophylactic peroneal nerve release and fasciotomy also were performed. After the self-lengthening nail has lengthened the leg through the osteotomy, the limb-length discrepancy is resolved. **E,** Lateral and **F,** AP view show that healing now can take place under the protection of the nail. (Reproduced with permission from the Rubin Institute for Advanced Orthopedics, Sinai Hospital of Baltimore, copyright 2009.)

associated with ankle equinus deformity and stiffness. Correction of the malunion must be accompanied by a simultaneous correction of the compensatory ankle equinus.

Limb-Length Discrepancy Correction

Limb-length discrepancy is common in malunions. To anticipate the length gain expected from the correction of the deformity, a radiograph should be taken in

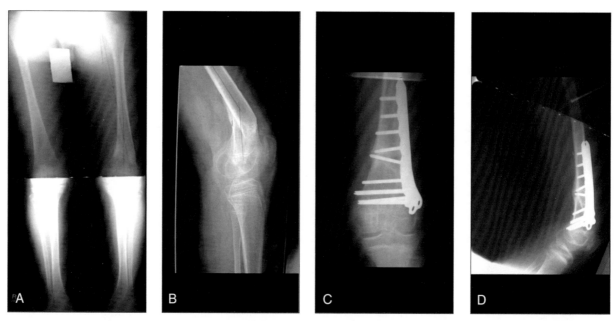

Figure 6 AP weight-bearing (**A**) and lateral (**B**) views of a 12-year-old boy with a distal left femur fracture treated in a cast with resulting malunion in varus and procurvatum. He was treated with closing wedge resection using fixator-assisted plating with locking plates as shown on these AP (**C**) and lateral (**D**) radiographic views. (Reproduced with permission from the Rubin Institute for Advanced Orthopedics, Sinai Hospital of Baltimore, copyright 2009.)

the plane of the maximum deformity (AP, lateral, or oblique). The length of the convex cortex of the involved bone should then be measured and compared with the normal side to predict the length gain anticipated from straightening. If straightening alone will not correct the discrepancy, then lengthening (simultaneous or staged) may be considered (Figure 5).

Treatment options for limb-length discrepancy include acute or gradual deformity correction. Gradual correction can be achieved only with external fixators. Acute correction can be achieved by internal or external fixation, but acute correction is more likely to put nerves and vessels at risk.[23,24] To achieve acute correction, the surgeon can perform a closing or opening wedge osteotomy with or without bone grafting (**Figure 6**). Restoration of length greater than 1 cm generally is not practical in acute corrections. Farquharson-Roberts[25] described a technique designed to correct both rotational malalignment and shortening after femoral shaft fractures treated with intramedullary nailing. Gradual lengthening is the mainstay for limb-length discrepancies in general,

however. Sangeorzan and associates[26] described a mathematically directed, single-cut osteotomy for the correction of tibial malunions that have both angular and rotational deformity. Other osteotomy techniques include a neutral wedge or dome-shaped osteotomy.

Fixation options for acute corrections include internal or external fixation. Internal fixation options include plates and screws, and locking intramedullary nails (with or without fixator assistance).[27,28] Internal fixation techniques are more invasive than external fixation techniques; in addition, external fixation allows adjustability and is therefore more "forgiving" than internal fixation (**Figures 7** and **8**). It is possible to obtain the advantages of both methods by using an external fixator as an intraoperative tool to hold the osteotomy in proper alignment, and applying a plate or nail for permanent fixation. Once the plate or nail is locked, the external fixator can be removed, so the patient never sees the external fixator. This method has been termed "fixator-assisted nailing" or "fixator-assisted plating."

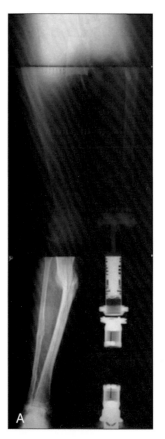

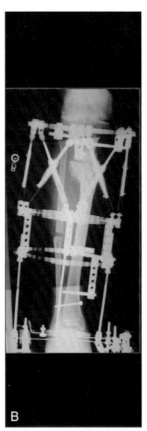

Figure 7 AP radiographs of a 64-year-old man with an above-knee amputation of the left leg and a malunited right tibia fracture in severe valgus, resulting in lateral compartment osteoarthritis. **A,** Before treatment. **B,** After treatment with tibial and fibular osteotomies and gradual correction with a six-axis, circular external fixator. The frame was removed 6 months later. (Reproduced with permission from the Rubin Institute for Advanced Orthopedics, Sinai Hospital of Baltimore, 2009.)

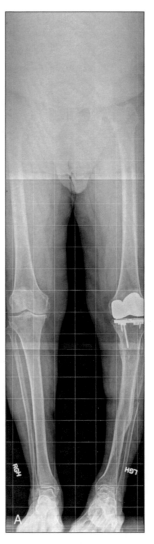

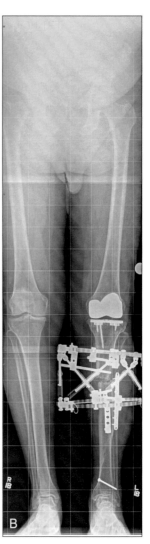

Figure 8 Weight-bearing AP radiographic views of a malunited tibial fracture of the left leg with a total knee arthroplasty of the ipsilateral knee. **A,** Before treatment. **B,** The malunion was treated with gradual correction using a six-axis, circular external fixator and a locking plate on the fibula. The frame was removed after 4 months. (Reproduced with permission from Paley D, Catagni MA, Argnani F, Villa A, Benedetti GB, Cattaneo R: Ilizarov treatment of tibial nonunions with bone loss. *Clin Orthop Relat Res* 1989;241:146-165.)

The disadvantages of external fixators are their bulk and inconvenience and the high likelihood of pin tract infections. Their superiority over internal fixators lies in their adjustability and their ability to gain length through distraction osteogenesis.

Bone Grafts and Bone Graft Substitutes

Bone grafts promote healing by providing osteogenic, osteoconductive, or osteoinductive activity.[29-31] An osteogenic material, such as autologous bone graft, contains living cells capable of forming bone. Autografts also have osteoinductive and osteoconductive properties. An osteoconductive material,

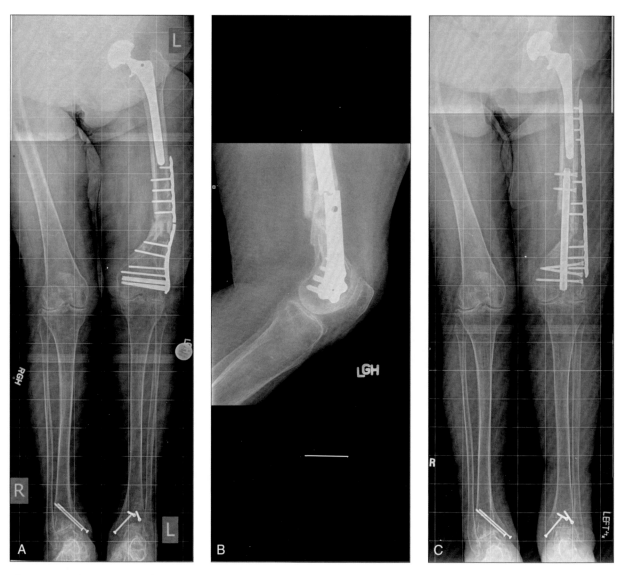

Figure 9 Mal-nonunion of a distal femur fracture of the left leg below a total hip arthroplasty. **A,** AP weight-bearing radiograph shows a severe varus deformity. **B,** Lateral sagittal view demonstrates a broken plate. **C,** AP weight-bearing view demonstrates the deformity after removal of all broken hardware, treatment with autologous bone grafting, BMP-2 insertion, and internal fixation with a retrograde supracondylar intramedullary nail and supplementary locked plate to neutralize the forces between the rod and the prosthesis. (Reproduced with permission from the Rubin Institute for Advanced Orthopedics, Sinai Hospital of Baltimore, copyright 2009.)

such as allogeneic bone graft, acts as a scaffold to promote the apposition of bone onto its surface. Allografts are neither osteoinductive nor osteogenic. An osteoinductive material has the biologic capacity to stimulate local or grafted cells to develop into osteoblasts. Bone morphogenetic protein (BMP) has such osteoinductive potential.[29] Demineralized and decalcified bone matrix (ie, type 1 collagen and noncollagenous proteins) contain osteoinductive growth factors (eg, BMPs) that act as both osteoinductive and osteoconductive factors.[30-32] Recombinant human BMP-7 (rhBMP-7, also known as osteogenic protein-1 [OP-1]) is effective in tibial nonunions. BMP-2 also has been used as an adjunct treatment in grade III open tibial fractures.[33,34] Jones and associates[35] showed that BMP-2 combined with allograft is equivalent in effectiveness to autograft in diaphyseal tibial fractures with cortical defects. **Figure 9** demonstrates a case in which autograft was used in addition to BMP-2.

Bone graft substitutes that have primarily osteoconductive properties include coralline hydroxyapatite, collagen-based matrices, calcium phosphate, calcium sulfate, and tricalcium phosphate.[36] Growth factors are present in platelets. Chiang and associates[37] studied the effects of using bone graft enriched with autologous platelet gel for recalcitrant nonunions. Autologous bone marrow injection has been used to treat nonunions based on its osteoinductive potential.[38]

Treatment Options for Nonunions

The goals of nonunion treatment are to obtain alignment, function, bone healing, and if infection is present, eradication of infection.[8] Circular external fixators and certain monolateral and hybrid fixators using Ilizarov principles can address all components of the deformity, including shortening. The circular external fixators not only achieve length, but also produce a correction that is gradual and gentle. Additionally, a compromised soft-tissue bed may accommodate the percutaneous wires and pins of an external fixator more easily than the extensive open exposure and implantation of an internal fixation plate.

Smoking has a negative effect on healing and increases complications. Giannoudis and associates[39] also observed that using nonsteroidal anti-inflammatory drugs after a fracture was associated with an increased incidence of nonunions.

Weight-bearing casts might stimulate the nonunion site by enhancing callus formation.[40] As in fractures treated with intramedullary nailing, dynamization of the nail may promote healing in nonunions by transferring the weight-bearing loads to the nonunion area.[41] Dynamization should be performed promptly (3 to 6 months after the injury) if signs of delayed union already exist.[10]

Exchange nailing may be preferred if the nonunion persists. The exchange nailing procedure consists of removing the existing nail, reaming the bone to a greater diameter, and inserting a larger diameter nail than the original.

Fibular osteotomy for tibial nonunions is performed to enhance the healing in the tibia. The fibula typically heals sooner than the tibia and becomes load sharing, reducing the actual loads through the tibial fracture site. Isolated fibular osteotomy should be reserved for those hypertrophic tibial nonunions with little or no deformity.[40]

Plate osteosynthesis offers enhanced stability for hypervascular nonunions and exposure for bone grafting in avascular nonunions. It also is preferred for proximal and distal metaphyseal juxta-articular nonunions, where intramedullary nailing would not offer sufficient fixation.[10] Minor angular deformities can be corrected by applying a plate under tension on the convex side of the bone.[42] Plate fixation has some limitations in the tibia, however, where soft-tissue coverage may be a concern. Plating is a load-bearing procedure, so patients are required to refrain from bearing weight after the surgery until healing occurs.[40]

External fixation is another alternative that offers good stability, correction of all components of a deformity, and added length.[43-45] It allows partial weight bearing, even in the immediate postoperative period. It also circumvents the need to violate the nonunion site and it does not preclude applying bone graft to the nonunion area.

Bone grafting should be considered when a concern exists about the vascularity and viability of the nonunion. Percutaneous bone marrow grafting allows delivery of osteoinductive bone marrow content to the nonunion site in a minimally invasive manner.[38,46,47]

Preventing Malunions and Nonunions

Malunions can be prevented by careful attention to detail in the initial reduction and fixation of the fracture. In minimally comminuted fractures, alignment is easy to see radiographically. In comminuted fractures

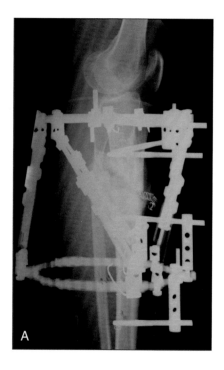

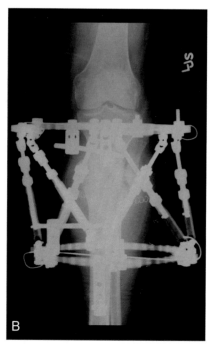

Figure 10 Mal-nonunion of the left proximal tibia in a 44-year-old woman after treatment with removal of the lateral plate, osteotomy of the fibula, resection of the tibial nonunion, an autologous bone graft harvested from the ipsilateral femoral canal, and application of a six-axis, circular external fixator. Lateral (**A**) and AP (**B**) radiographs demonstrate the good bone apposition at the nonunion site using an external fixator. Note the proper alignment of the tibia following the resection of the nonunion. (Reproduced with permission from the Rubin Institute for Advanced Orthopedics, Sinai Hospital of Baltimore, copyright 2009.)

or fractures with bone loss, however, alignment is less obvious. To achieve alignment in such cases, we apply a temporary external fixator, which can be checked during surgery with radiographs or by using a cautery cord extended from hip to ankle, under image intensification. The definitive internal fixation is then applied, and the temporary external fixator is removed. Alternatively, adjustable external fixation may be used as the definitive fixation. This option permits changes and adjustments in the postoperative period.

Nonunions can be prevented by careful handling of soft tissues, minimal stripping of periosteum, stable fixation, and early bone grafting. Addressing risk factors, such as smoking and the use of nonsteroidal anti-inflammatory medications, also contributes to the prevention of nonunions.

CASE MANAGEMENT AND OUTCOME SUMMARY

Our initial treatment of the 44-year old woman described earlier consisted of optimizing her preoperative condition through counseling about the adverse effects of smoking on bone healing. Because of the patient's psychiatric history, a preoperative social work consult also was arranged to ensure that the patient would be able to comply reliably with all the postoperative instructions and office visits.

Our treatment of the nonunion included percutaneous removal of the lateral plate, osteotomy of the fibula, resection of the tibial nonunion, an autologous bone graft harvested from the ipsilateral femoral canal, and application of a six-axis, circular external fixator. The nonunion was resected through a transverse anterior incision overlying the prominent proximal anterior tibia, which allowed excellent access to the bone and allowed the skin edges to reapproximate easily after the bone resection. Once the proximal and distal bone ends were resected sharply with an oscillating saw, the nonunion was very mobile and the deformity could be corrected acutely. A high-speed burr also was used to débride all remaining bone to clean, healthy, bleeding bone.

Another crucial step in the preparation of the nonunion repair was opening the sclerotic bone ends of the tibia with a drill. This step allowed healthy intramedullary bone marrow to connect with the nonunion. The intramedullary bone graft from the ipsilateral femur was harvested before the resection of the nonunion through a percutaneous approach using an intramedullary reamer-irrigator-aspirator system at the level of the greater trochanter. The bone graft then was placed temporarily in a covered container while the nonunion was prepared.

The bone graft was inserted into the nonunion site with the addition of concentrated BMP-2 to induce bone formation. The skin was then closed, and the six-axis, circular external fixator was applied to the bone and used to realign the bone segments acutely. Postoperative radiographs showed anatomic alignment (**Figure 10**).

Postoperatively, the patient began physical therapy, to maintain range of motion of the knee and ankle, and gait training, with weight bearing as tolerated. Office visits initially were scheduled every 2 weeks so that an additional 3 to 4 mm of compression to the nonunion could be applied in the office as needed. The external fixator was maintained for 3 months, until the patient could walk comfortably without any assistive device and radiographs demonstrated evidence of healing. The fixator was then "dynamized" in the office, in anticipation of fixator removal under anesthesia 1 month later.

This case highlights some of the dilemmas associated with a proximal tibial nonunion, made even more challenging in a patient who smokes. The initial reduction of the fracture must have been difficult, as indicated by the antikick plate used at the time of the initial rodding and by the bending of the rod, which indicated that a small rod was used initially. Additionally, a rod was not the ideal type of fixation for this very proximal fracture. The lateral plating surgery also represented a less-than-ideal choice because lateral plates do a poor job of stabilizing the fracture in the plane of the deforming forces (the patellar tendon and the gastrocnemius muscles), causing the proximal piece to extend and the distal piece to flex (known as apex anterior bowing). The external fixator chosen for the definitive fixation in this case neutralized these deforming forces by placing fixation anteriorly. The external fixator also can provide adjustable, rigid fixation with good pin spread and divergence.

The oblique shape of the bone ends also predisposed the fracture to inherent instability. The shear at the fracture interface was corrected when the bone ends were squared off during preparation of the nonunion bed. The square bone ends allowed the bone to be compressed longitudinally without shear in a much more stable fashion than in the original surgery, thus imparting internal stability, which complemented the external stability provided by the fixator. The external fixator corrected the alignment of the leg and also could be used to maintain compression to the nonunion in the postoperative setting. The external fixator also allowed the patient to bear weight immediately. Immediate weight bearing was especially important for this patient because of her psychiatric disorder, which could have affected her potential postoperative compliance. Had a plate been used, it would have been necessary to restrict weight bearing to a much greater extent.

The nonunion was atrophic, as evidenced by its gross mobility (>15°) at the initial clinical presentation. The atrophic nonunion was treated with resection of the atrophic bone ends to healthy, bleeding bone. Opening the medullary canals of the proximal and distal tibia also facilitated the bone-healing environment so that normal bone marrow could bathe the nonunion in healthy cells. This procedure might have been enough to promote healing in this patient, but, because she was a smoker, an autologous bone grafting procedure augmented with BMP-2 was performed to promote optimal healing.

After fixator removal and rehabilitation, the patient regained full function of her leg. Healing was achieved despite the presence of two significant risk factors: smoking and schizophrenia.

STRATEGIES FOR MINIMIZING COMMON COMPLICATIONS

In conclusion, the surgeon should select the best tools to treat the nonunion, depending on the type of nonunion, the condition of the bone and soft-tissue coverage, the size and position of the bone fragments, the level of the nonunion, and the size of any bony defect.[41] Most important, the surgeon should select tools and strategies that work best in his or her hands. Treatment must be individualized to produce the best outcome for each patient.

Nonunions and malunions can be prevented in most cases. The initial fracture surgery should be performed with careful attention to reproducing normal anatomic and mechanical alignment. In the presence of risk factors for nonunion—such as smoking, bone loss, or systemic illness—additional steps can be taken proactively. For example, early bone grafting, external bone stimulation, and smoking cessation may all reduce the risk of developing a nonunion. Nonunions and malunions are best prevented rather than treated. Once established as problems, careful surgical planning and implementation are crucial to a successful outcome.

REFERENCES

1. Zalavras CG, Patzakis MJ: Open fractures: Evaluation and management. *J Am Acad Orthop Surg* 2003;11(3):212-219.

2. Probe RA: Lower extremity angular malunion: Evaluation and surgical correction. *J Am Acad Orthop Surg* 2003;11(5):302-311.

3. Milner SA, Davis TR, Muir KR, Greenwood DC, Doherty M: Long-term outcome after tibial shaft fracture: Is malunion important? *J Bone Joint Surg Am* 2002;84-A(6):971-980.

4. McKellop HA, Sigholm G, Redfern FC, Doyle B, Sarmiento A, Luck JV Sr: The effect of simulated fracture-angulations of the tibia on cartilage pressures in the knee joint. *J Bone Joint Surg Am* 1991;73(9): 1382-1391.

5. Tetsworth K, Paley D: Malalignment and degenerative arthropathy. *Orthop Clin North Am* 1994;25(3): 367-377.

6. van der Schoot DK, Den Outer AJ, Bode PJ, Obermann WR, van Vugt AB: Degenerative changes at the knee and ankle related to malunion of tibial fractures. 15-year follow-up of 88 patients. *J Bone Joint Surg Br* 1996;78(5):722-725.

7. Merchant TC, Dietz FR: Long-term follow-up after fractures of the tibial and fibular shafts. *J Bone Joint Surg Am* 1989;71(4):599-606.

8. Rosen H: Treatment of nonunions: General principles, in Chapman MW (ed): *Operative Orthopaedics*. Philadelphia, PA, Lippincott, 1993, pp 749-769.

9. La Velle DG: Delayed union and nonunion of fractures, in Canale ST (ed): *Campbell's Operative Orthopaedics*, ed 9. St. Louis, MO, Mosby-Year Book, 1998, pp 2579-2599.

10. Lynch JR, Taitsman LA, Barei DP, Nork SE: Femoral nonunion: Risk factors and treatment options. *J Am Acad Orthop Surg* 2008;16(2):88-97.

11. Bhattacharyya T, Bouchard KA, Phadke A, Meigs JB, Kassarjian A, Salamipour H: The accuracy of computed tomography for the diagnosis of tibial nonunion. *J Bone Joint Surg Am* 2006;88(4):692-697.

12. Goulet JA, Bray TJ: Nonunions and malunions of the tibia, in Chapman MW (ed): *Operative Orthopaedics*. Philadelphia, PA, Lippincott, 1993, pp 855-870.

13. Weber BG, Čech O: *Pseudarthrosis: Pathology, Biomechanics, Therapy, Results*. Hans Huber, Bern, Switzerland, 1976.

14. Rozbruch SR, Herzenberg JE, Tetsworth K, Tuten HR, Paley D: Distraction osteogenesis for nonunion after high tibial osteotomy. *Clin Orthop Relat Res* 2002;394(394):227-235.

15. Paley D, Chaudray M, Pirone AM, Lentz P, Kautz D: Treatment of malunions and mal-nonunions of the femur and tibia by detailed preoperative planning and the Ilizarov techniques. *Orthop Clin North Am* 1990;21(4):667-691.

16. Bhargava A, Paley D, Herzenberg JE, Shah S: Distraction treatment for hypertrophic nonunions. *Orthop Trans* 1996;20:135.

17. Catagni MA, Guerreschi F, Holman JA, Cattaneo R: Distraction osteogenesis in the treatment of stiff hypertrophic nonunions using the Ilizarov apparatus. *Clin Orthop Relat Res* 1994;301(301):159-163.

18. Paley D, Herzenberg JE, Tetsworth K, McKie J, Bhave A: Deformity planning for frontal and sagittal plane corrective osteotomies. *Orthop Clin North Am* 1994;25(3):425-465.

19. Paley D: Frontal plane mechanical and anatomic axis planning, in *Principles of Deformity Correction*. Springer, Berlin, Germany, 2002, pp 61-98.

20. Paley D: Osteotomy concepts and frontal plane realignment, in *Principles of Deformity Correction*. Springer, Berlin, Germany, 2002, pp 99-154.

21. Green SA, Gibbs P: The relationship of angulation to translation in fracture deformities. *J Bone Joint Surg Am* 1994;76(3):390-397.

22. Paley D: Oblique plane deformities, in *Principles of Deformity Correction*. Springer, Berlin, Germany, 2002, pp 175-194.

23. Knight JL, Ratcliffe SS, Weber JK, Hansen ST Jr: Corrective osteotomy of femoral shaft malunion causing complete occlusion of the superficial femoral artery. *J Bone Joint Surg Am* 1980;62(2):303-306.

24. Johnson EE: Acute lengthening of shortened lower extremities after malunion or non-union of a fracture. *J Bone Joint Surg Am* 1994;76(3):379-389.

25. Farquharson-Roberts MA: Corrective osteotomy for combined shortening and rotational malunion of the femur. *J Bone Joint Surg Br* 1995;77(6):979-980.

26. Sangeorzan BJ, Sangeorzan BP, Hansen ST Jr, Judd RP: Mathematically directed single-cut osteotomy for correction of tibial malunion. *J Orthop Trauma* 1989;3(4):267-275.

27. Eralp L, Kocaoglu M, Cakmak M, Ozden VE: A correction of windswept deformity by fixator assisted nailing. A report of two cases. *J Bone Joint Surg Br* 2004;86(7):1065-1068.

28. Marsh DR, Shah S, Elliott J, Kurdy N: The Ilizarov method in nonunion, malunion and infection of fractures. *J Bone Joint Surg Br* 1997;79(2):273-279.

29. Bauer TW, Muschler GF: Bone graft materials. An overview of the basic science. *Clin Orthop Relat Res* 2000;371(371):10-27.

30. Finkemeier CG: Bone-grafting and bone-graft substitutes. *J Bone Joint Surg Am* 2002;84-A(3):454-464.

31. Gazdag AR, Lane JM, Glaser D, Forster RA: Alternatives to autogenous bone graft: Efficacy and indications. *J Am Acad Orthop Surg* 1995;3(1):1-8.

32. Bolander ME, Balian G: The use of demineralized bone matrix in the repair of segmental defects. Augmentation with extracted matrix proteins and a comparison with autologous grafts. *J Bone Joint Surg Am* 1986;68(8):1264-1274.

33. Govender S, Csimma C, Genant HK, et al: BMP-2 Evaluation in Surgery for Tibial Trauma (BESTT) Study Group: Recombinant human bone morphogenetic protein-2 for treatment of open tibial fractures: a prospective, controlled, randomized study of four hundred and fifty patients. *J Bone Joint Surg Am* 2002; 84-A(12):2123-2134.

34. Swiontkowski MF, Aro HT, Donell S, et al: Recombinant human bone morphogenetic protein-2 in open tibial fractures. A subgroup analysis of data combined from two prospective randomized studies. *J Bone Joint Surg Am* 2006;88(6):1258-1265.

35. Jones AL, Bucholz RW, Bosse MJ, et al: BMP-2 Evaluation in Surgery for Tibial Trauma-Allograft (BESTT-ALL) Study Group: Recombinant human BMP-2 and allograft compared with autogenous bone graft for reconstruction of diaphyseal tibial fractures with cortical defects. A randomized, controlled trial. *J Bone Joint Surg Am* 2006;88(7):1431-1441.

36. Hak DJ: The use of osteoconductive bone graft substitutes in orthopaedic trauma. *J Am Acad Orthop Surg* 2007;15(9):525-536.

37. Chiang CC, Su CY, Huang CK, Chen WM, Chen TH, Tzeng YH: Early experience and results of bone graft enriched with autologous platelet gel for recalcitrant nonunions of lower extremity. *J Trauma* 2007;63(3):655-661.

38. Hernigou P, Poignard A, Beaujean F, Rouard H: Percutaneous autologous bone-marrow grafting for nonunions. Influence of the number and concentration of progenitor cells. *J Bone Joint Surg Am* 2005;87(7):1430-1437.

39. Giannoudis PV, Dinopoulos H, Tsiridis E: Bone substitutes: An update. *Injury* 2005;36(Suppl 3):S20-S27.

40. Wiss DA, Stetson WB: Tibial nonunion: Treatment alternatives. *J Am Acad Orthop Surg* 1996;4(5):249-257.

41. Wu CC, Shih CH: A small effect of weight bearing in promoting fracture healing. *Arch Orthop Trauma Surg* 1992;112(1):28-32.

42. Rodriguez-Merchan EC, Gomez-Castresana F: Internal fixation of nonunions. *Clin Orthop Relat Res* 2004;419(419):13-20.

43. Brinker MR, O'Connor DP: Outcomes of tibial nonunion in older adults following treatment using the Ilizarov method. *J Orthop Trauma* 2007;21(9):634-642.

44. Rozbruch SR, Pugsley JS, Fragomen AT, Ilizarov S: Repair of tibial nonunions and bone defects with the Taylor Spatial Frame. *J Orthop Trauma* 2008;22(2):88-95.

45. Patil S, Montgomery R: Management of complex tibial and femoral nonunion using the Ilizarov technique, and its cost implications. *J Bone Joint Surg Br* 2006;88(7):928-932.

46. Connolly JF, Guse R, Tiedeman J, Dehne R: Autologous marrow injection as a substitute for operative grafting of tibial nonunions. *Clin Orthop Relat Res* 1991;266(266):259-270.

47. Garg NK, Gaur S, Sharma S: Percutaneous autogenous bone marrow grafting in 20 cases of ununited fracture. *Acta Orthop Scand* 1993;64(6):671-672.

Chapter 7

INFECTION FOLLOWING OPEN FRACTURE

George Cierny III, MD

CASE PRESENTATION

History

A 25-year-old man sustained a high-energy, segmental, Gustilo IIIB open fracture of the right tibia while racing an all-terrain vehicle in Mexico. Initial treatment consisted of débridement and temporary stabilization with an external fixator and administration of systemic antibiotics. On postoperative day 5, he underwent fixation with a locked intramedullary nail and delayed closure. By 3 weeks, the wound had suppurated and subsequently dehisced. The soft tissues were débrided and intravenous antibiotics were administered for 4 weeks.

The patient returned to the United States at 8 weeks postinjury with the fracture site and hardware exposed. Culture swabs of the wound failed to grow pathogens. The patient was empirically given an oral first-generation cephalosporin and instructions to stop smoking, remain on partial weight bearing, and change his dressings twice daily.

After the patient spent 3 additional months at home, a new fistula formed just above the ankle, and shortly thereafter, the distal locking screws suppurated, extruded, and cultured positive for *Pseudomonas aeruginosa*. The patient was started on oral sulfamethoxazole and trimethoprim. After 6 weeks, the leg had shortened and become unstable and painful. Six months after injury, the patient had two reasonable options: ablation or limb salvage. In either case, the wound would require a complete excision.

Current Problem and Initial Management

The patient was evaluated at our center 9 months after the initial injury. His right leg was 2 cm shorter than the contralateral leg and deformed. All soft-tissue compartments were firm, tender, and indurated. Four fistulas were seen along the medial border of the distal leg, two just above the ankle and two within the initial traumatic wound. Dead bone, the fracture site, and the

---

Dr. Cierny or an immediate family member is a member of a speakers' bureau or has made paid presentations on behalf of Kimberly Clark and owns stock or stock options in Royer Biomedical.

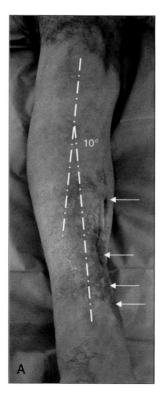 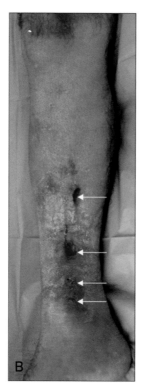 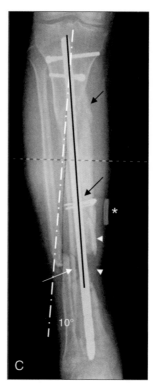 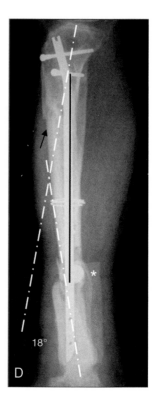

Figure 1 Images of a 25-year-old man who sustained a Gustilo IIIB fracture of the right tibia that led to a stage IV osteomyelitis. Anterior (**A**) and lateral (**B**) clinical photographs of the right leg demonstrating varus angulation (dotted and dashed lines) and the presence of four fistulas (arrows) draining from within a surgical scar above the medial ankle. AP (**C**) and lateral (**D**) radiographs revealing a comminuted fracture stabilized with a locked intramedullary nail. The two more proximal fractures (black arrows) had healed in varus and procurvatum (white dotted and dashed lines) to the mechanical axis (black lines); the distalmost segment was not united to the shaft and was fixed in 18° of procurvatum to the mechanical axis. Also apparent were a 3.5-cm cortical defect (white arrow) and fractures through two separate end-cortical sequestra (white arrowheads). The asterisks (*) indicate silver-impregnated gauze dressings.

intramedullary nail were exposed (**Figure 1**, *A* and *B*). All three pulses were intact per Doppler, and sensation to the foot was intact. Radiographs (**Figure 1**, *C* and *D*) revealed a segmental, comminuted fracture of the right tibia stabilized with the intramedullary nail abutting subchondral bone at the ankle plafond. The fibula fracture was overlapped approximately 2 cm. Two more proximal fractures had healed in 10° of varus and 10° of procurvatum with 1.3-cm medial translation. At the distal metaphyseal-diaphyseal junction, the tibia was still not united through a 3.5-cm cortical defect and two end-cortical sequestra. In addition, the distalmost segment was fixed in an additional 8° of procurvatum to the shaft and had

two large cortical defects from the previously extruded locking screws. Additional radiographs were ordered to confirm that the ankle joint had not been violated by the tip of the nail. An arteriogram showed a three-vessel run-off to the foot but significant tethering of the anterior bundle, presumably due to shortening. The patient had stopped smoking, reversing the smoking-related systemic compromise.[1]

DISCUSSION

Open fractures create the "perfect storm" for infection to complicate injury: the initial wound is con-

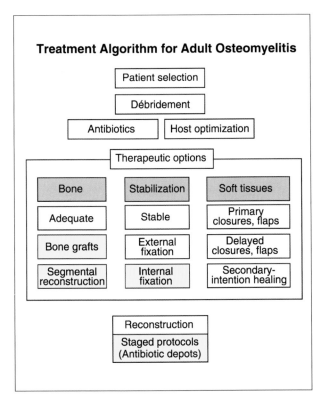

Treatment Algorithm for Adult Osteomyelitis

Patient selection

Débridement

Antibiotics   Host optimization

Therapeutic options

Bone	Stabilization	Soft tissues
Adequate	Stable	Primary closures, flaps
Bone grafts	External fixation	Delayed closures, flaps
Segmental reconstruction	Internal fixation	Secondary-intention healing

Reconstruction
Staged protocols (Antibiotic depots)

Figure 2   Universal treatment algorithm for acute and chronic osteomyelitis, based on a live, clean, manageable wound following débridement. Three wound parameters (gray boxes) drive the reconstruction: the integrity of the bony segment, the relative need for stabilization, and the quality of the soft-tissue envelope. The need for a bone graft implies a segment at risk for insufficiency fracture, whereas a segmental defect mandates an intercalary reconstruction. The yellow boxes designate procedures best staged to follow a course of local antibiotic therapy. Secondary-intention healing is used only for small wounds or in the absence of large, surgical implants or grafts. (Adapted with permission from Cierny GC III, DiPasquale D: Adult osteomyelitis, in Cierny GC III, McClaren AC, Wongworawat MD, eds: *Orthopaedic Knowledge Update: Musculoskeletal Infection*. Rosemont, IL, American Academy of Orthopaedic Surgeons, 2009, p 138.)

taminated, and injury to soft tissues potentiates an ongoing exposure to pathogens; surgical implants and dead bone fragments grant safe haven to proliferating microbes; ischemia, dead space, and foreign bodies impede local immunity and the delivery of antibiotics; and shock, injury, and preexisting health conditions compromise the host response. The goals of treatment are threefold: timely intervention; creation and maintenance of a clean, manageable wound; and adequate and durable fracture fixation (**Figure 2**).

Early in the course of infection following fracture, microorganisms are mobile (planktonic) and yet vulnerable to antibiotics and host defenses. If the fracture fragments are live and stable, the infection may resolve after a clean wound is established by adequate wound decompression, antimicrobial therapy, and the elimination of dead space.[2-6] After 4 weeks, however, reactions between surface macromolecules occur at pathogen-substrate interfaces, resulting in a resilient microzone of attachment, which serves as a precursor to a microbial-based, mucopolysaccharide

"slime," or biofilm, that encompasses the entire colony. At this point, the host will have lost the "race for the surface."[7] Within this biofilm, microbial nutrition and growth are enhanced and microbes are protected from host defenses and penetration by antimicrobials.[7] The result is a profound compromise to the host: wound healing and fracture repair are impaired as a result of the toxins produced by the pathologens and the by-products of the host's unsuccessful efforts to destroy the biofilm colony. Curative treatment requires the surgical removal of the entire biofilm burden and antimicrobial therapy.

When infection complicates the management of open fracture injuries, the spectrum of treatment parallels the fundamental principles and mechanisms inherent to wound colonization by microorganisms. The format and complexity of treatment depend on the presence of surgical implants, the extent of osteonecrosis, the time since injury or contamination, and the overall health of the patient.[8] Further distinction must be made between infections with microscopic (minimal) osteonecrosis versus those with

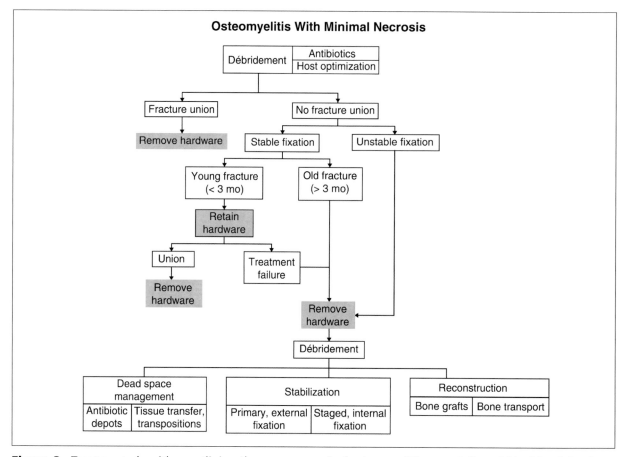

Osteomyelitis With Minimal Necrosis

Figure 3 Treatment algorithm outlining the management of osteomyelitis types I, II, and IV with minimal necrosis and indwelling hardware. Factors influencing decision making include the status of the fracture union, the adequacy of fixation and alignment, the biologic capacity of the fracture to heal, and the ability to optimize a host response. Hardware is simply removed in osteomyelitis lesions with minimal necrosis types I and II. In type IV lesions, the quality of fixation and the time since injury guide the selection of treatment. The temporal distinctions of "young" and "old" designate the remaining capacity of the fracture to unite, given opportunity.

macroscopic osteonecrosis. In micronecrosis, necrotic soft tissues and surgical implants serve as a nidus for the infection (osteomyelitis with minimal necrosis). In osteomyelitis with macronecrosis, large bony sequestra compound the complexity of treatment.[8] Because of these considerations, I prefer to use the terms "early" and "late" to describe biofilm formation and the terms "young" and "old" to describe fracture healing, in place of the older terms, such as "acute" and "chronic" in treatment algorithms crafted to parallel milestones in the natural history of this disease (**Figure 3**).

Recognizing Infection Following Open Fracture

The medical and surgical history, physical examination, and diagnostic laboratory screening will disclose the site and source of infection, the time lapsed since injury, and most systemic host comorbidities. The erythrocyte sedimentation rate (ESR) and C-reactive protein (CRP) level are the most reliable indices for detecting both early and late infections. Clinical signs and symptoms of vascular insufficiency will guide the use of angiography, sonography, and transcutaneous

TABLE 1   Host Factors Affecting Osteomyelitis Treatment Outcomes

Local Factors
Arteritis
Venous stasis
Chronic edema
Radiation fibrosis
Extensive scarring
Large-vessel disease

Systemic Factors
Hypoxia
Malignancy
Malnutrition
Extremes of age
Substance abuse
Inhibitory drugs
Colonization
Resistant pathogens
Diabetes
Organ failure
Obesity
Tobacco use
Immune deficits

Adapted with permission from Cierny G III: Classification and treatment of adult osteomyelitis, in Everts CM, ed: *Surgery of the Musculoskeletal System*, ed 2. New York, NY, Churchill Livingstone, 1990, vol 5, pp 4337-4379.

oxygen tensions when planning to manipulate soft tissues for coverage and considering alternate methods of fixation. Imaging modalities are used selectively: plain radiographs disclose hardware, alignment, healing, and stability; MRI and nuclear scans help define the zone of injury; and CT highlights bony architecture and occult healing disturbances.[9,10]

Treatment outcomes are adversely affected by the underlying medical conditions of the host. Health-compromised patients are at risk because of metabolic disturbances, a high incidence of skin and wound breakdown, immune deficiencies, frequent episodes of bacteremia, and excessive bleeding (**Table 1**), and the effects of these deficiencies are cumulative.[11-13] Local factors are predictive of vascular compromise to wound healing, whereas systemic factors affect the metabolic, hematopoetic, and immune status of the host. To improve treatment outcomes in the at-risk patient, precautions are taken to promote optimization of the host response throughout treatment.

Preoperative reversal of wound-healing deficiencies will improve treatment outcomes to levels similar to those of healthy patients.[1,14]

The risk of failure also can be reduced by choosing treatments with low morbidity. For an infected nonunion of the tibia with soft-tissue loss, low-risk surgery would include a below-knee amputation and external fixation of an acute limb shortening.[15] Free flaps and internal fixation with bone grafts are morbid, high-risk procedures. Nevertheless, when reconstruction does call for a surgical implant, the risk of failure can be reduced by staging the reconstruction to follow pretreatment with an antibiotic depot (**Figure 2**). This additional treatment step safeguards the provision for wound coverage while reducing the strain on host defenses to clear out residual pathogens before the final reconstruction.[16-18]

To identify the pathogens responsible for the infection, multiple deep-tissue samples must be obtained and cultured.[19,20] Intraoperative frozen sections are used to differentiate bacterial infection from other diseases (granulomatous infections, tumors). If a neoplasm is discovered, additional tissue is collected for processing. The laboratory is asked to set up aerobic and anaerobic cultures, mycobacterial acid-fast bacillus or fungal cultures (if granulomas are discovered), and vortex-sonication cultures if implants are removed.[21]

Managing Infection Following Open Fracture
Antibiotic Therapy

Once adequate tissue samples have been secured and processed, broad-spectrum systemic antibiotic coverage is initiated. Thereafter, coverage is tailored to the sensitivities of the organisms isolated from the wound. Initial coverage for fungi or mycobacterium is based on the clinical history, suspicion, or frozen sections; cultures for these organisms may take weeks to verify. Ideal antibiotic coverage maintains a 1:1 ratio between the mean inhibitory concentration (MIC) and mean bactericidal concentration (MBC) of the pathogen. Serum concentrations are kept at a level at least 6 times the MBC.[22] Oral or intravenous delivery may be administered safely providing the agents are bactericidal and cover all wound isolates.

After débridement, significant numbers of planktonic bacteria and microscopic fragments of the biofilm colony (sessile organisms) will persist despite copious wound lavage. The high levels of antimicrobial agents concentrated in a wound seroma following implantation of an antibiotic depot are capable of killing all pathogen phenotypes.[16-18,23-25] Only high-dose antibiotic composites can push the elution kinetics to establish and maintain the concentrations needed to reliably eliminate sessile pathogens. Aside from the single line of commercially available gentamicin-loaded joint-spacers, the customary use of local antibiotic depots to treat infection is currently limited in the United States to handmade antibiotic beads and spacers.[26-29] Commercially prepared, antibiotic-impregnated bone cements incorporate low-dose antibiotics and are intended only for prophylaxis.[30] Antibiotic-loaded implants may be left as permanent implants, removed, or exchanged for bone grafts or hardware at a later date.

Polymethylmethacrylate (PMMA) is the most common material used to create antibiotic beads and spacers. Biodegradable calcium sulfate beads obviate any concerns about leaving acrylic depots in situ as foreign bodies. However, these resorbable products have their own drawbacks: the antibiotics that can be mixed successfully into the kits are limited; and a 25% rate of spontaneous fistula formation has been reported with the use of antibiotic-loaded resorbable calcium sulfate beads, due in part to the voluminous and inflammatory by-products of degradation.[29]

Although many different types of open fracture injuries occur, osteomyelitis typically develops in one of four anatomic patterns: type I, medullary osteomyelitis; type II, superficial osteomyelitis; type III, localized osteomyelitis; and type IV, diffuse osteomyelitis.[8] The infection can be early or late, stable or unstable, and refractory or responsive to suppressive therapy. Patients are categorized according to their health status or anticipated gain from therapy: healthy patients (A-hosts), patients with wound-healing deficiencies affecting outcomes (B-hosts), and patients for whom the risks of treatment outweigh the potential benefits (C-hosts). In the latter category, palliation is the goal rather than treatment or cure. The anatomic type of infection is combined with the patient's host classification to designate one of twelve clinical stages (eg, stage IA, stage IIIC, stage IVB), which can then be used to assess outcomes when comparing treatment protocols.

Suppressive therapy is reserved for young, or immature, wounds (< 3 months) with minimal tissue necrosis, adequate stability, acceptable alignment, and residual potential for fracture consolidation, ie, type IV osteomyelitis with minimal necrosis.[31] Wide-margined amputations are indicated when functional restoration or palliation is neither safe nor feasible. Limb-salvage protocols must, therefore, offer distinct outcome advantages over palliation, suppression, or amputation to justify patient exposure to the risks of treatment.

Osteomyelitis With Minimal Necrosis

Osteomyelitis can occur with either minimal necrosis or macronecrosis. Osteomyelitis with minimal necrosis occurs when the bone is exposed to infection but no bony sequestra are present to contribute to the biofilm burden.[8] The bone is live and does not serve as a nidus for the infectious process (**Figures 4** and **5**). Instead, the source of infection is often the exposure of dead space and hardware from the loss of wound coverage. An example of this type of osteomyelitis would be an infection that occurs following internal fixation and closure of a low-energy open fracture. The bone is live but not necessarily clean or stable. Anatomic types of osteomyelitis with minimal necrosis include types I, II, and IV. By definition, no type III osteomyelitis with minimal necrosis exists because no macrocortical sequestra are found in this category of disease.

The choice of treatment should be based on the time since contamination, the status of the fracture, the quality of the fixation, and the medical condition of the host. The first two factors are discussed more fully below.

Time Since Contamination

Early osteomyelitis with minimal necrosis (< 4 weeks). Because a fracture does not unite by 4 weeks, all early osteomyelitis with minimal necrosis lesions are, by definition, type IV osteomyelitis (diffuse and intrinsically unstable). The medullary canal is involved as in type I, and soft-tissue coverage is often deficient as in type II. Surgical fixation implants are

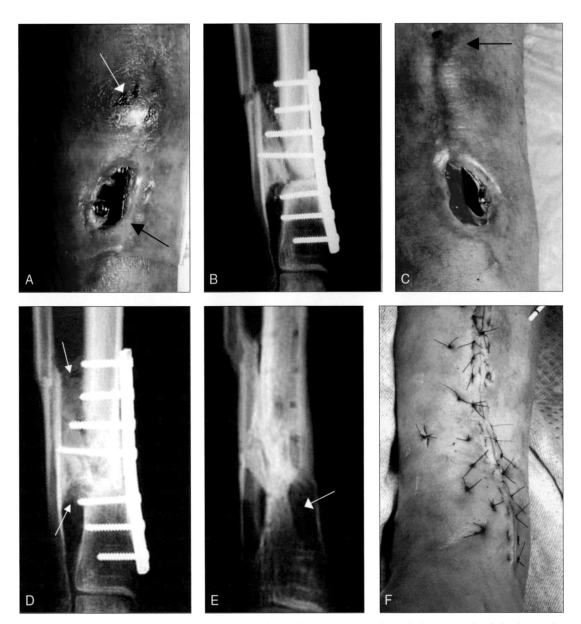

Figure 4   Images of a low-energy open fracture of the distal tibia. **A,** Clinical photograph of the lower leg 9 weeks after plate fixation and cancellous grafting of a nonunion. Hardware is exposed (black arrow) and a new fistula is forming (white arrow). **B,** AP radiograph showing solid plate fixation of the nonunion with good alignment and cross-fixation to the fibula. The medical history, low-energy nature of the injury, and radiographic assessment designate this wound a biofilm infection with minimal bony necrosis, loss of coverage, and colonization of the exposed hardware. Because fixation was rigid, the bone was live, and the reduction was early (< 3 months), a suppression protocol was initiated in an attempt to gain union prior to a débridement and hardware removal. **C,** After the patient had 12 weeks of rest, smoking cessation, hyperbaric oxygen treatment, and systemic antibiotics, the wound was no longer inflamed and the new fistula had resolved (arrow); **D,** AP radiograph demonstrating consolidation of the grafts (arrows), synostosis with the fibula, and union across the fracture site. **E,** At 4 months, the hardware was removed and the cortex beneath it was débrided (arrow). **F,** The wound margins were then advanced and closed over thin antibiotic-impregnated calcium sulfate wafers.

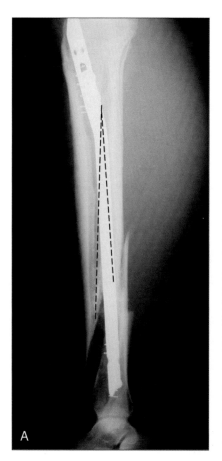
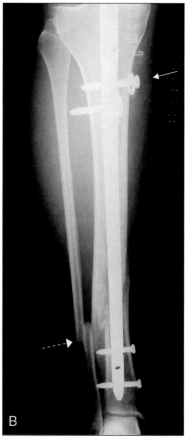

Figure 5 Images of early type IVA osteomyelitis of the tibia with minimal necrosis. **A,** Lateral radiograph of the affected limb 3 weeks after locked-rod fixation of the low-energy, spiral fracture of the distal tibia. Fixation and reduction were inadequate because of a displaced, coronal fracture of the shaft (dashed lines), which had complicated attempts at intramedullary fixation. **B,** AP radiograph showing 2 cm of shortening (dashed arrow) and loosening of the proximalmost locking screw (solid arrow). **C,** Clinical photograph taken at the time of admission. The limb is erythematous and edematous, and a draining fistula (arrow) overlies the loose screw seen in **B.** After 48 hours of elevation and intravenous antibiotics, the hardware was removed, the canal was reamed, and the resulting dead space was filled with antibiotic-loaded calcium sulfate beads that contained vancomycin and tobramycin.

commonly present. The goals of treatment are to control the infection and to promote union. To accomplish these goals, adequate fracture fixation and reduction are important considerations: instability will add further injury, perpetuate infection, and prevent union; and malalignment may herald early fixation failure, prolong disability, and limit treatment options.[32,33] Reasons for treatment failure include severe host compromise, the presence of unrecognized or resistant pathogens, inadequate antibiotic therapy, or an occult nidus of infection,

such as thermal necrosis of the bone or indwelling hardware.[2-6]

In stable conditions, when fixation and alignment are adequate, treatment can focus on the débridement, the delivery of antimicrobials, elimination of dead space, and, when indicated, durable wound closure. Following procurement of adequate tissue cultures, bactericidal antibiotics are initiated and the débridement is taken to viable margins. The wound may then be left open or sealed in an antibiotic bead pouch for delayed coverage.[34] Primary closures are performed in

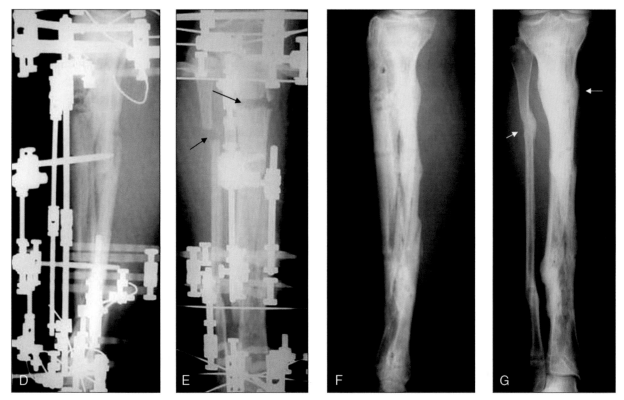

Figure 5   D, AP radiograph demonstrating the reduction and stabilization of the fractures using a ring fixator and the Ilizarov method. **E,** AP radiograph demonstrating the restoration of limb length through proximal corticotomies (arrows). AP **(F)** and lateral **(G)** radiographs taken at 2-year follow up demonstrate union of the fractures, consolidation of the regenerate bone (arrows), and adequate restoration of the mechanical axis. At 5-year follow-up, the patient remains infection free.

conjunction with local antibiotic depots to eliminate residual pathogens, maintain workable dead space, and safeguard closure.[35,36] If the fracture site is stable but deficient, the depot can be exchanged for bone grafts or fixation devices during a later procedure.

Although a live wound will eventually heal by secondary intention, open wounds pose obstacles to treatment. The components of the reconstruction must themselves be live to withstand ongoing contamination. Long-standing colonization of exposed implants can lead to fixation failure. Early wound coverage, on the other hand, is crucial when vital structures are exposed or when biofilm formation must be prevented to create new opportunities for treatment (**Figure 6**).

In unstable conditions, when fracture fixation or reduction is inadequate from the beginning, a new treatment protocol is indicated. Existing hardware is removed and all tissues are débrided to viable margins. The new method of fixation must address bony deficiencies and long-term stability while preserving the blood supply of the remaining fracture fragments. External fixation is safe to use after nearly all attempts at fixation. Internal fixation is best managed in a two-stage protocol, following coverage and a course of antibiotic beads.[27,37,38] To preserve the vitality of diaphyseal cortices, exchanging intramedullary fixation for plate fixation (and vice versa) is discouraged.

Late osteomyelitis with minimal necrosis (> 4 weeks). After 4 weeks, a mature biofilm colony will have formed on exposed substrate surfaces.[7] Although débridement and closure over indwelling hardware is no longer an option, suppression of the infection and host support to union is an acceptable alternative to

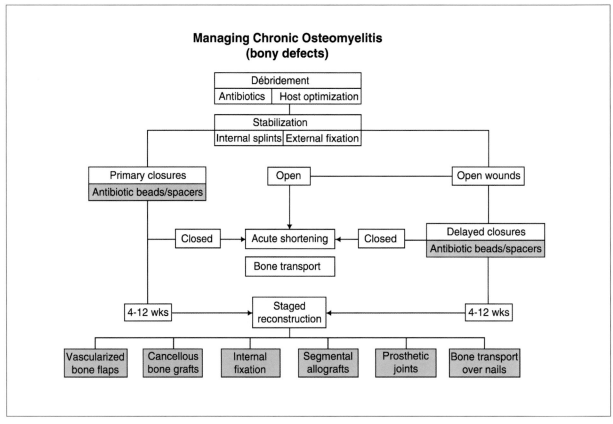

Figure 6 Treatment algorithm illustrating how restoration of the soft tissues increases reconstruction options when treating large, bony débridement defects. A supple wound closure and pretreatment with an antibiotic depot (gray boxes) will safeguard the use of internal fixation devices, large bone grafts, and prosthetic components (blue boxes). Acute shortenings and open bone transport are the only methods compatible with protocols calling for healing by secondary intention. (Adapted from Cierny G III, DiPasquale D: Treatment of chronic infection. *J Am Acad Orthop Surg* 2006;14(10):105-110.)

a new treatment protocol in select circumstances. The presence or absence of union and the quality of fracture fixation will guide patient selection and treatment (**Figure 3**).

Fracture Status

Type I osteomyelitis with minimal necrosis. The fracture is healed and the infection is limited to the endosteum. The soft tissues are usually adequate, and a history or presence of intramedullary fixation is common. Treatment calls for removal of hardware and sequential débridement of the canal by reaming or through a cortical window (unroofing).[8] Residual dead space is managed with a closed suction drain or

an antibiotic depot, which is the preferred method. The duration of systemic antibiotic coverage will vary according to the methods used: 1 week for antibiotic depots; 2 to 4 weeks for closed suction drainage.[8,27]

Type II osteomyelitis with minimal necrosis. The fracture is united, bone and hardware are exposed, and the soft-tissue envelope is deficient (**Figure 4**). Treatment requires resection of soft tissues to viable margins, hardware removal, and tangential débridement of cortical surfaces. Coverage can be primary or delayed, or the wound can be left to heal by secondary intention. Systemic antibiotics are continued for 7 to 10 days.[27,39]

Type IV osteomyelitis with minimal necrosis. The fracture is not united, the endosteum is exposed to the infectious process, soft tissues may be deficient, and hardware is often present (**Figure 5**). The choice of treatment is based on the time since injury, the quality of the reduction, and the quality of fracture fixation.[25] If the reduction is reasonable and fracture healing is still biologically feasible (because the fracture occurred within the previous 3 months), suppression to union may be the best treatment. In the later cases (less than 3 months), every effort must be made to identify and sensitivity test wound pathogens because bactericidal antibiotic therapy is essential to a successful outcome.[40] If, however, the fracture is older than 3 months, the fracture fixation is unacceptable, or the opposing bone ends are atrophic on radiographs, débridement, hardware removal, and a new osteosynthesis are indicated (**Figure 3**).

Osteomyelitis With Macronecrosis

Classic, chronic osteomyelitis infections occur with macronecrosis and are usually sequelae of high-energy, open trauma. They include anatomic types I through IV, a significant element of dead bone, and a B-host cohort of > 50%.[1,8] Restoration of the soft-tissue envelope is difficult because most lesions have an extended zone of injury. Bone loss and focal defects from previous fixation complicate the design of new fixation strategies. Treatment is based on the time since injury, the anatomic site, the condition of the host, the risks of treatment, and institutional resources.

Time Since Injury

Early type IV osteomyelitis (< 4 weeks). When infection is associated with macroscopic osteonecrosis and is diagnosed within 4 weeks of injury, timely intervention will often obviate initiation of a new treatment.[35,36] Early type IV osteomyelitis is treated as a planktonic rather than as a biofilm infection and is similarly triaged according to the quality of the fracture fixation/reduction (**Figure 3**). After a thorough débridement, attention is turned to the elimination of dead space, wound perfusion, coverage, and delivery of antibiotics to all potential substrate surfaces. These goals are most commonly achieved with the combined use of systemic antibiotics, local antibiotic depots, and adjacent versus remote tissue transfers. If, however, the fracture is unstable or malaligned, a new treatment protocol is indicated (**Figure 2**).

Late type IV osteomyelitis (> 4 weeks). After more than 4 weeks of growth, the biofilm colony is well established. Treatment will require the elimination of all implants, foreign bodies, and sequestra (**Figure 6**). If curative treatment would be too morbid for host tolerance or the proposed reconstruction is without sufficient benefit to the patient, ablative and palliative therapies become the preferred methods of treatment. The approach to limb salvage begins with an intralesional, wide excision of the inflammatory process. All nonviable and ischemic tissues are resected to viable margins; cortical bone is débrided to surfaces with normal, Haversian bleeding (the "paprika sign").[41-42] Frozen sections are used to confirm normal marrow margins because incomplete excision of the biofilm burden will lead to treatment failure.[8,43-46] Thereafter, the débridement site is lavaged and prepared for stabilization and subsequent wound management.

Anatomic Types

Medullary osteomyelitis (type I). The fracture has united. Although draining fistulas are not uncommon, the overall soft-tissue envelope is usually uncompromised. Treatment is similar to that described for late type I osteomyelitis with minimal necrosis. If a history or presence of medullary fixation exists, care must be taken to ascertain the viability of previously reamed surfaces to avoid a missed biofilm nidus following thermal injury.

Superficial osteomyelitis (type II). The fracture has united and a full-thickness defect is present in the soft-tissue envelope, exposing surfaces of dead bone and internal fixation devices. Although the treatment of this type of osteomyelitis is similar to that described for type II osteomyelitis with minimal necrosis, the extended zone of injury associated with late osteomyelitis with macronecrosis often rules out closure using local tissue transposition following débridement or hardware removal (**Figure 4**, *E* and *F*).[47] For similar reasons, healing by secondary intention is discouraged. Distant tissue transfer (free flaps) is the most common method used to provide coverage.[37,38,43,48]

Localized osteomyelitis (type III). This type is characterized by the presence of a full-thickness, cortical sequestrum. The fracture has united, and elements of type I and type II osteomyelitis are often present. The dead bone fragments are usually endcortical or triangular "butterfly" pieces intimately associated with fracture callus or involucrum. Treatment requires sequestrectomy. If the bone remaining after débridement is expected to be adequate to withstand the stresses of daily activity, management of the residual dead space will be simplified with use of soft tissue or antibiotic depots. If, however, the remaining bone is expected to be at risk for insufficiency fracture, either stabilization is provided before débridement with use of an external fixator or a bypass bone graft, or an in situ reconstruction is staged to follow coverage and local antibiotic therapy (**Figures 2** and **3**).[42,49,50]

Diffuse osteomyelitis (type IV). The infection contains elements common to all the other anatomic types. In this anatomic classification, instability is paramount. Usually the original fracture site is not united. However, diffuse osteomyelitis also includes stress or iatrogenic fractures within the same zone of injury and healed fractures in which a type I, II, or III nidus will, upon débridement, lead to instability (eg, an infected union with supracondylar sequestration of the distal femur). Limb salvage will, therefore, require further fixation by either continued external fixation or a staged internal method. Dead space management will include methods of compression-distraction as well as methods used to treat types I, II, and III.[51,52]

Composite bony and soft-tissue reconstructions are complicated and time consuming and are best managed with multistaged protocols.[31,53,54] First, dead space is eliminated with an antibiotic depot and the wound is then covered. At the second stage, the depot is removed and the bony defect is reconstructed as a clean surgical procedure (**Figure 1**). Once the risk of cross-contamination has been eliminated, the surgeon can safely choose any reconstructive technique (**Figure 6**).[55] Treatment options depend on the condition of the host, the anatomic site, and the resources available to the health-care team. With experience and the careful matching of technique to case-specific parameters, success rates should be similar for all reconstructive techniques, including vascularized bone flaps,[1,56] bone trans-

port,[57] revision total joint arthroplasties,[11,28] and bone grafting within titanium cages.[58]

Preventing the Problem

To harness the potential benefit of a suppression protocol, the antibiotic coverage must be both continuous and bactericidal and must cover all wound pathogens. Cultures taken from the surfaces of a biofilm infection using tissue swabs often yield too few planktonic bacteria to grow adequately. Most of the colony is sessile (biofilm-bound) and unavailable for culture. Multiple tissue specimens provide significantly larger numbers of planktonic organisms and should have been taken once the initial report had come back showing no growth. This patient's protocol ultimately failed, in part, because of inadequate coverage for *Pseudomonas*, which in turn led to hardware failure, deformity, and instability.

CASE MANAGEMENT AND OUTCOME SUMMARY

By the time the patient described earlier had returned to the United States, he had a late (> 4 weeks) stage IVB osteomyelitis of the tibia with macronecrosis. His fractures were young (< 3 months), reduced, and stable (**Figure 3**), qualifying him for entry into an antibiotic suppression protocol to avoid immediate débridement and hardware removal while the fractures healed. Cessation of smoking eliminated a significant compromise to wound healing, thereby improving the patient's prognosis through host optimization. Although suppression ultimately failed before union, two of the three tibial fractures healed, thereby reducing the complexity of the retreatment at our center.

The patient was compromised locally (a B^L host) because of an extended zone of injury to all compartments and fracture fragments. On evaluation, it was clear that he would have a significant bone and soft-tissue defect after débridement.

A left free fibula graft with a skin paddle was believed to be the best way to eliminate both defects. Vascularized bone would heal even in a compromised wound bed. All three donor vessels were avail-

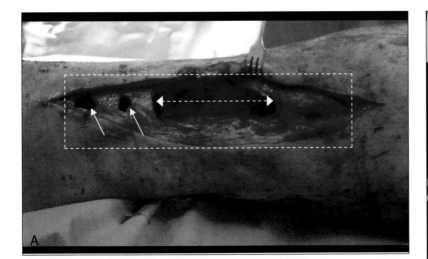

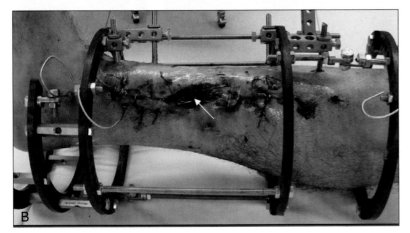

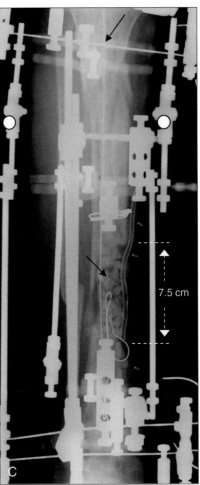

Figure 7   Images of the 25-year-old man described in the case presentation after initial treatment at my institution. **A,** Clinical photograph demonstrating the 7.5-cm cortical defect (dashed arrow) and 14.5-cm x 4.5-cm soft-tissue defect (box) that were created at débridement. The distal screw holes (white arrows) were enlarged to débride the distalmost canal. **B,** Clinical photograph demonstrating the application of an Ilizarov frame and the live wound that was sealed within an antibiotic bead pouch (arrow). **C,** AP radiograph of the defect (dotted white lines/arrow) and the entire canal, which were filled with antibiotic beads (black arrows). Alignment was corrected through proximal offset hinges (white circles), and lengthening took place through the distal resection site.

able, making an ideal, end-to-end anastomosis possible. Fixation by a multiplanar external fixator was the most logical choice for both stabilization and deformity correction. Other methods were not as attractive, for the following reasons: bone transport using a split, traumatized segment (diaphysis) was too risky; the wound was too ischemic to support a large bone graft; acute shortening was unsafe because of compromise to the anterior vessels and the size of the anticipated defect; and a myoplasty transposition in this location would prove inade-

quate to contain a bead-seroma or facilitate reconstruction.

The initial débridement led to a 7.5-cm bony and 14-cm x 4.5-cm soft-tissue deficit (**Figure 7,** A). The canal was reamed and the distal metaphysis unroofed through the old screw sites. The wound was loosely approximated and the residual defect was sealed within an antibiotic bead pouch (**Figure 7,** B). The dead space and pouch were filled with antibiotic-impregnated PMMA beads, and an Ilizarov external fixator was applied to stabilize, realign, and lengthen

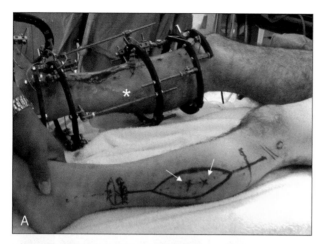

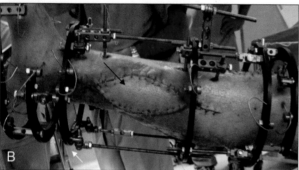

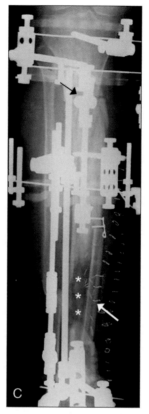

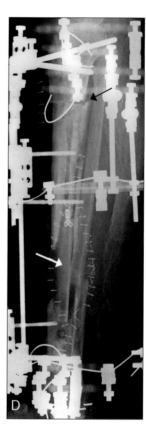

Figure 8 Images of the 25-year-old man showing later treatment. **A,** Clinical photograph taken before transferring the donor skin paddle from the left fibula to the right extremity. Access to the donor vessels was facilitated by leaving a window (asterisk) in the medial aspect of the frame. The donor skin paddle has been sketched on the left leg (foreground). The two Xs within the paddle (arrows) mark the sounding of two septal perforators from the peroneal artery. **B,** Clinical photograph of the fibular skin paddle (arrow) sutured into place on the right limb after successful anastamosis to posterior vessels. AP (**C**) and lateral (**D**) radiographs showing the fibular graft in position (white arrows), the proximal corticotomy (black arrows), and restoration of the tibial axis. Cancellous bone grafts (asterisks) were placed lateral to the free fibula graft and across the intraosseous membrane to affect a synostosis with the ipsilateral fibula.

the tibia (**Figure 7,** *C*). Intraoperative cultures grew *P aeruginosa*, multiple anaerobic bacteria, and an oxacillin-sensitive *Staphylococcus aureus*.

On day 4 after débridement, the PMMA beads were removed and replaced with biodegradable calcium sulfate beads containing vancomycin, piperacillin sodium, and tazobactam sodium. A corticotomy was performed through the proximalmost fracture site to correct the anatomic axis. Length was restored through the resection defect, and the wound was again dressed with a bead pouch.

On day 13, once the axis and limb length had been restored, a vascularized free fibula flap with skin

paddle was transferred from the left leg to restore the right leg (**Figure 8,** *A* and *B*). Cancellous bone grafts, harvested from the left iliac crest, were used to supplement the transfer and to perform an osteosynostosis with the ipsilateral fibula (**Figure 8,** *C* and *D*).

SUMMARY

The process by which an acute infection becomes chronic parallels time-related mechanisms inherent to microbial colonization of wound surfaces. Knowing how much time has lapsed since the index inoculation with microorganisms is, therefore, useful in selecting treatment options. In the early setting (< 4 weeks), treatment has three goals: elimination of dead space, wound perfusion, and prevention of further injury. To accomplish these goals, a competent soft-tissue envelope is often critical for a successful outcome.

After 4 weeks, the situation changes. Surviving pathogens transform into a biofilm colony, immune to both antimicrobials and host defenses. At this point, the factors that drive treatment selection are the extent of the necrosis (minimal necrosis versus macronecrosis), the time since injury (age of the fracture), and the status of the fracture fixation (stable versus unstable). If a new protocol must be initiated, the mechanical demands of the site, the condition of the host, the risks of treatment, and the experience of the health care team will determine both the methods and outcomes of treatment.

STRATEGIES FOR MINIMIZING COMPLICATIONS

To minimize the development of complications from infection, patients should be followed closely after treatment: All wound drainage should be cultured and treated. Blood samples should be serially checked through CBC, ESR, and CRP. Wound healing disturbances should be managed early and aggressively, especially in B hosts and in wounds with dead bone fragments or indwelling hardware.

When treating infection following open fracture, antimicrobial therapy should be based on the results of deep-tissue cultures, not swabs. Antibiotics that are bactericidal for all wound pathogens should be prescribed. The host's response should be optimized throughout treatment.

It also is important to remember the biologic distinctions between early (< 4 weeks) and late (> 4 weeks) infections and to treat them accordingly. The time since injury (less than or more than 3 months) should be used to guide suppressive versus curative treatment when managing late type IV osteomyelitis lesions with minimal necrosis. Low-risk methods should be used in high-risk patients to improve treatment outcomes.

REFERENCES

1. Cierny G III, DiPasquale D: Treatment of chronic infection. *J Am Acad Orthop Surg* 2006;14(10 Spec No.):S105-S110.

2. Burger RR, Basch T, Hopson CN: Implant salvage in infected total knee arthroplasty. *Clin Orthop Relat Res* 1991;273:105-112.

3. Hartman MB, Fehring TK, Jordan L, Norton HJ: Periprosthetic knee sepsis. The role of irrigation and debridement. *Clin Orthop Relat Res* 1991;273: 113-118.

4. Khoury AE, Lam K, Ellis B, Costerton JW: Prevention and control of bacterial infections associated with medical devices. *ASAIO J* 1991;38:174-178.

5. Crockarell JR Jr, Hanssen AD, Osmon DR, Morrey BF: Treatment of infection with débridement and retention of the components following hip arthroplasty. *J Bone Joint Surg Am* 1998;80(9):1306-1313.

6. Davis N, Curry A, Gambhir AK, et al: Intraoperative bacterial contamination in operations for joint replacement. *J Bone Joint Surg Br* 1999;81(5):886-889.

7. Gristina AG: Biomaterial-centered infection: Microbial adhesion versus tissue integration. *Science* 1987;237(4822):1588-1595.

8. Cierny G III, Mader JT, Penninck JJ: A clinical staging system for adult osteomyelitis. *Clin Orthop Relat Res* 2003;414:7-24.

9. Erdman WA, Tamburro F, Jayson HT, Weatherall PT, Ferry KB, Peshock RM: Osteomyelitis: Characteristics and pitfalls of diagnosis with MR imaging. *Radiology* 1991;180(2):533-539.

10. Gross T, Kaim AH, Regazzoni P, Widmer AF: Current concepts in posttraumatic osteomyelitis: A diagnostic challenge with new imaging options. *J Trauma* 2002;52(6):1210-1219.

11. McPherson EJ, Tontz WT Jr, Patzakis M, et al: Outcome of infected total knee utilizing a staging system for prosthetic joint infection. *Am J Orthop* 1999;28(3):161-165.

12. Cierny G III, DiPasquale D: Periprosthetic total joint infections: Staging, treatment, and outcomes. *Clin Orthop Relat Res* 2002;403:23-28.

13. Lai K, Bohm ER, Burnell C, Hedden DR: Presence of medical comorbidities in patients with infected primary hip or knee arthroplasties. *J Arthroplasty* 2007;22(5):651-656.

14. Emori TG, Gaynes RP: An overview of nosocomial infections, including the role of the microbiology laboratory. *Clin Microbiol Rev* 1993;6(4):428-442.

15. Cierny G III, Rao N: Procedure-related reduction of the risk of infection, in Cierny G, McClaren A,

Wongworawat DM (eds): *OKU: Musculoskeletal Infection.* Rosemont, IL, American Academy of Orthopaedic Surgeons, 2009; pp 43-53.

16. Walenkamp GH: *Gentamicin PMMA Beads: A Clinical, Pharmacokinetic and Toxicologic Study.* Amsterdam, The Netherlands: Drukkerij Cliteur,1983; pp 19-22.

17. Ostermann PA, Seligson D, Henry SL: Local antibiotic therapy for severe open fractures. A review of 1085 consecutive cases. *J Bone Joint Surg Br* 1995;77(1): 93-97.

18. Engesaeter LB, Lie SA, Espehaug B, Furnes O, Vollset SE, Havelin LI: Antibiotic prophylaxis in total hip arthroplasty: Effects of antibiotic prophylaxis systemically and in bone cement on the revision rate of 22,170 primary hip replacements followed 0-14 years in the Norwegian Arthroplasty Register. *Acta Orthop Scand* 2003;74(6):644-651.

19. Perry CR, Pearson RL, Miller GA: Accuracy of cultures of material from swabbing of the superficial aspect of the wound and needle biopsy in the preoperative assessment of osteomyelitis. *J Bone Joint Surg Am* 1991;73(5):745-749.

20. Patzakis MJ, Wilkins J, Kumar J, Holtom P, Greenbaum B, Ressler R: Comparison of the results of bacterial cultures from multiple sites in chronic osteomyelitis of long bones. A prospective study. *J Bone Joint Surg Am* 1994;76(5):664-666.

21. Kobayashi N, Bauer TW, Tuohy MJ, Fujishiro T, Procop GW: Brief ultrasonication improves detection of biofilm-formative bacteria around a metal implant. *Clin Orthop Relat Res* 2007;457:210-213.

22. Cierny G III, Mader JT: The surgical treatment of adult osteomyelitis, in Evarts C, McCollister MD (eds): *Surgery of the Musculoskeletal System*, ed. 1. New York, NY, Churchhill Livingston, 1983; pp 4814-4834.

23. Wahlig H, Dingeldein E, Bergmann R, Reuss K: The release of gentamicin from polymethylmethacrylate beads. An experimental and pharmacokinetic study. *J Bone Joint Surg Br* 1978;60-B(2):270-275.

24. Adams K, Couch L, Cierny G III, Calhoun J, Mader JT: In vitro and in vivo evaluation of antibiotic diffusion from antibiotic-impregnated polymethylmethacrylate beads. *Clin Orthop Relat Res* 1992;278:244-252.

25. Zalavras CG, Patzakis MJ, Holtom P: Local antibiotic therapy in the treatment of open fractures and osteomyelitis. *Clin Orthop Relat Res* 2004;427:86-93.

26. Paley D, Herzenberg JE: Intramedullary infections treated with antibiotic cement rods: Preliminary results in nine cases. *J Orthop Trauma* 2002;16(10):723-729.

27. Cierny G III: Chronic osteomyelitis: results of treatment. *Instr Course Lect* 1990;39:495-508.

28. Younger AS, Duncan CP, Masri BA: Treatment of infection associated with segmental bone loss in the proxi-

mal part of the femur in two stages with use of an antibiotic-loaded interval prosthesis. *J Bone Joint Surg Am* 1998;80(1):60-69.

29. McKee MD, Wild LM, Schemitsch EH, Waddell JP: The use of an antibiotic-impregnated, osteoconductive, bioabsorbable bone substitute in the treatment of infected long bone defects: Early results of a prospective trial. *J Orthop Trauma* 2002;16(9):622-627.

30. Hanssen AD: Local antibiotic delivery vehicles in the treatment of musculoskeletal infection. *Clin Orthop Relat Res* 2005;437:91-96.

31. Patzakis MJ: Management of acute and chronic osteomyelitis, in Chapman MW, Szabo RM, Marder RA, et al (eds): *Chapman's Orthopaedic Surgery.* Philadelphia, PA, Lippincott Williams and Wilkins, 2000, pp 3533-3559.

32. Merritt K, Dowd JD: Role of internal fixation in infection of open fractures: Studies with Staphylococcus aureus and Proteus mirabilis. *J Orthop Res* 1987;5(1):23-28.

33. Worlock P, Slack R, Harvey L, Mawhinney R: The prevention of infection in open fractures: an experimental study of the effect of fracture stability. *Injury* 1994;25(1):31-38.

34. Henry SL, Ostermann PA, Seligson D: The prophylactic use of antibiotic impregnated beads in open fractures. *J Trauma* 1990;30(10):1231-1238.

35. Cierny G III, Byrd HS, Jones RE: Primary versus delayed soft tissue coverage for severe open tibial fractures. A comparison of results. *Clin Orthop Relat Res* 1983;178:54-63.

36. Bhattacharyya T, Mehta P, Smith M, Pomahac B: Routine use of wound vacuum-assisted closure does not allow coverage delay for open tibia fractures. *Plast Reconstr Surg* 2008;121(4):1263-1266.

37. Cierny G III, Nahai F: Soft tissue reconstruction of the lower leg: Part I. *Perspect Plast Surg* 1988;1(1):1-32.

38. Cierny G III, Nahai F: Dialogue: Lower extremity reconstruction: Part II. *Perspect Plast Surg* 1988;1(2):76-78.

39. Swiontkowski MF, Hanel DP, Vedder NB, Schwappach JR: A comparison of short- and long-term intravenous antibiotic therapy in the postoperative management of adult osteomyelitis. *J Bone Joint Surg Br* 1999;81(6):1046-1050.

40. Court-Brown CM, Keating JF, McQueen MM: Infection after intramedullary nailing of the tibia. Incidence and protocol for management. *J Bone Joint Surg Br* 1992;74(5):770-774.

41. Sachs BL, Shaffer JW: Osteomyelitis of the tibia and femur: A critical evaluation of the effectiveness of the Papineau technique in a prospective study. Paper #214, presented at the 50th Annual Meeting of the American

Academy of Orthopaedic Surgeons, Anaheim, CA, 1983.

42. Harmon PJ: A simplified surgical approach to the posterior tibia for bone grafting and fibular transference. *J Bone Joint Surg Am* 1945;27:496-498.

43. Damholt VV: Treatment of chronic osteomyelitis: A prospective study of 55 cases treated with radical surgery and primary wound closure. *Acta Orthop Scand* 1982;53(5):715-720.

44. Lorat-Jacob A, Guiziou B, Ramadier JO: Fractures Infectees de Jambe. *Rev Chir Orthop Repar Appar Mot* 1985;71:515-526.

45. Esterhai JL Jr, Sennett B, Gelb H, et al: Treatment of chronic osteomyelitis complicating nonunion and segmental defects of the tibia with open cancellous bone graft, posterolateral bone graft, and soft-tissue transfer. *J Trauma* 1990;30(1):49-54.

46. Simpson AH, Deakin M, Latham JM: Chronic osteomyelitis. The effect of the extent of surgical resection on infection-free survival. *J Bone Joint Surg Br* 2001;83(3):403-407.

47. Pollak AN, McCarthy ML, Burgess AR: The Lower Extremity Assessment Project (LEAP) Study Group: Short-term wound complications after application of flaps for coverage of traumatic soft-tissue defects about the tibia. *J Bone Joint Surg Am* 2000;82-A(12):1681-1691.

48. Gayle LB, Lineaweaver WC, Oliva A, et al: Treatment of chronic osteomyelitis of the lower extremities with debridement and microvascular muscle transfer. *Clin Plast Surg* 1992;19(4):895-903.

49. Campanacci M, Zaanoli S: Double tibio-fibular synostosis (fibula pro tibia) for non-union and delayed union of the tibia: End result review of one hundred seventy-one cases. *J Bone Joint Surg Am* 1966;48:44-56.

50. Fodor L, Ullmann Y, Soudry M, Calif E, Lerner A: Prophylactic external fixation and extensive bone debridement for chronic osteomyelitis. *Acta Orthop Belg* 2006;72(4):448-453.

51. Betz AM, Hierner R, Baumgart R, et al: Primary shortening—secondary lengthening. A new treatment concept for reconstruction of extensive soft tissue and bone injuries after 3rd degree open fracture and amputation of the lower leg (German). *Handchir Mikrochir Plast Chir* 1998;30(1):30-39.

52. Sen C, Kocaoglu M, Eralp L, Gulsen M, Cinar M: Bifocal compression-distraction in the acute treatment of grade III open tibia fractures with bone and soft-tissue loss: A report of 24 cases. *J Orthop Trauma* 2004;18(3):150-157.

53. Cierny G III: The classification and treatment of adult osteomyelitis, in Evarts CM: *Surgery of the Musculoskeletal System*, ed 2. New York, NY, Churchill Livingstone, 1990.

54. Cierny G III: Infected tibial nonunions (1981-1995). The evolution of change. *Clin Orthop Relat Res* 1999;360:97-105.

55. Cierny G, DiPasquale D: Chronic Osteomyelitis, in Cierny G, McClaren A, Wongworawat DM (ed.): *OKU: Musculoskeletal Infection*. Rosemont, IL, American Academy of Orthopaedic Surgeons, 2009.

56. Yajima H, Tamai S, Mizumoto S, Inada Y: Vascularized fibular grafts in the treatment of osteomyelitis and infected nonunion. *Clin Orthop Relat Res* 1993;293:256-264.

57. Cierny G III, Zorn KE: Segmental tibial defects. Comparing conventional and Ilizarov methodologies. *Clin Orthop Relat Res* 1994;301:118-123.

58. Cobos JA, Lindsey RW, Gugala Z: The cylindrical titanium mesh cage for treatment of a long bone segmental defect: Description of a new technique and report of two cases. *J Orthop Trauma* 2000;14(1):54-59.

INDEX

Page numbers followed by *f* indicate figures; page numbers followed by *t* indicate tables.